The Trail Guide
to **GLACIER**
NATIONAL PARK

Erik Molvar

FALCON PRESS®

ACKNOWLEDGMENTS

This guide would not have been possible without the years of excellent service put in by the rangers with whom I had the pleasure of dealing. I would like to thank Mr. Jack Potter, GNP Backcountry Supervisor, for his editorial input throughout the writing of this book. I also thank Nancy Hoffman and Tom Habecker, former Glacier rangers, for their helpful comments and suggestions concerning the guide. Clyde Lockwood of the Glacier Natural History Association provided the initial assistance in dealing with publishing firms, and I am grateful for his continued support of my efforts.

—*Erik Molvar*

Falcon Press is continually expanding its list of recreational guidebooks using the same general format as this book. All books include detailed descriptions, accurate maps, and all information necessary for enjoyable trips. You can order extra copies of this book and get information and prices for other Falcon books by writing Falcon Press, P.O. Box 1718, Helena, MT 59624. Also, please ask for a free copy of our current catalog.

Library of Congress Catalog Card Number: 92-52701
ISBN: 1-56044-141-0

Printed in the United States of America.

All text, maps, and photos by the author except as noted.
Cover photo: Backpacking in Glacier National Park.
Photo by Michael S. Sample.

Recycled Paper

This book is dedicated to Sandy Staskus and Hope Brayton.
No one could ask for finer hiking partners.

CONTENTS

LOCATION OF TRAILS

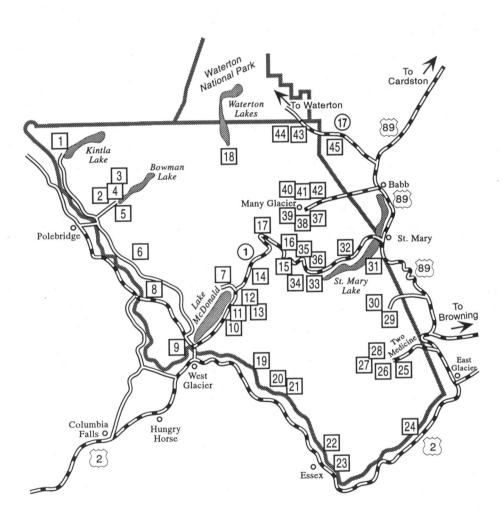

N

Waterton National Park

Waterton Lakes

To Cardston

To Waterton

Kintla Lake

Bowman Lake

Polebridge

Many Glacier

St. Mary

Babb

St. Mary Lake

Lake McDonald

West Glacier

Columbia Falls

Hungry Horse

Two Medicine

East Glacier

To Browning

Essex

0   5   10

miles

MAP LEGEND

MAP LEGEND:

Trail Described	⊖- - - - - -	Main Highway	
Alternate Trail	⊖- - - - - -	Improved Gravel Rd	
Cross Country Trail	------------	Jeep Road	= = = = =
National Park	▬▬▬▬▬	Ranger Station	
Country Boundaries	—-—-—	Visitor Center	
Falls/Rapids	~~//~	Lookout	□
River/Creeks	~~~	Campground	Λ
Lakes		Picnic Area	
Glacier		Pass	) (
Meadow		Mountain	▲▲
Mine		Tunnel	II

Backpacking toward Mt. Gould. Photo by Michael S. Sample.

INTRODUCTION

Glacier National Park was created in 1910 to preserve over one million acres of unspoiled wilderness. More than 730 miles of trail in the park provide access to soaring peaks and verdant forests, mountain meadows and fish-filled lakes—truly a backpacker's paradise. Here hikers have the opportunity to leave the hectic pace of "civilization" far behind and seek a form of refuge in the silent grandeur of the mountains. Tragically, most of the visitors to Glacier National Park never stray far from their automobiles, but those few adventurous souls who do plunge into the wilderness discover a wealth of natural beauty around every turn of the trail.

Natural History

Geology. The rock strata of Glacier National Park was laid down more than a billion years ago as sediment on the bottom of an inland sea. The oldest layer is of buff-colored Altyn limestone, with subsequent layers of greenish Appekuny argillite and reddish Grinnell argillite being deposited on top as mudstone and sandstone. Tectonic forces brought enormous pressure on the strata in this area, causing them to fold upward and eventually break. After the break, the forces continued, forcing a huge slab of rock to slide eastward a distance of forty-two miles over neighboring strata. This geologic feature is known as the Lewis Overthrust, and it is responsible for creating the original mountain masses of the park.

During the last Great Ice Age, continual heavy snowfall collected in pockets and valleys and compressed under its own weight to form glaciers. These glaciers began to move downhill, pulled by the forces of gravity. As they moved, they carved the rock of the valley walls and floors, scouring deep U-shaped trenches with natural amphitheaters, or *cirques*, at their heads. When the glaciers retreated, they left behind piles of debris called *lateral moraines* (along the sides of valleys) and *terminal moraines* (where the foot of the glacier had been). Terminal moraines formed natural dams in many cases, creating some of the many lakes that dot the park. The action of glaciers on the mountains has resulted in horn peaks and aretes. The action of later, smaller glaciers has carved smaller indentations, or *hanging cirques*, high on the walls of the original valleys. The remnants of these later glaciers remain active in many parts of the park.

Biological communities. Glacier National Park is a healthy, functioning system of communities that supports a wide variety of interdependent plant and animal species. At the end of the last Ice Age, temperatures at lower elevations began to rise. This encouraged faster-growing plants, and pushed cold weather-loving flora like relict tundra communities to higher elevations. As a result, an increase in elevation brings the hiker into communities that are very similar to those that dominate the subarctic and arctic regions. The lowlands reflect the convergence of a wide variety of plant communities—cedar-hemlock assemblages from the Pacific Northwest, grassland communities from the Great Plains, and fire-dependent lodgepole pine forests from the Rockies. The widely divergent plant communities that coexist in the park showcase a great diversity of animal species in a relatively small area.

Logan Creek and Mt. Reynolds.

USING THE GUIDE

This guide provides information that will help hikers choose backpacking trips according to their available time and abilities. It also gives a detailed description of the trail system and interprets natural features found along the trails. Use this guide in conjunction with topographic maps, which can be purchased at the St. Mary or Apgar visitor centers, local gift and sporting goods stores, or through the U.S. Geological Survey, Denver, CO 80225. The 1:100,000 scale topo map of the entire park gives a general impression of the landforms that will be encountered, and 1:24,000 scale quadrangle maps are available for those desiring greater detail. The appropriate quadrangle maps are listed for each major hike in the guide.

Each trail description begins with a quick and easy reference section outlining the physical characteristics of the trail. The outline includes distances (in miles and kilometers), the hike type (day hike or backpack), altitude gain and loss, appropriate topo maps, and degree of difficulty. The difficulty rating can be interpreted as follows: *Easy* trails can be completed without difficulty by hikers of all abilities; *Moderate* hikes will challenge novices; *Moderately Strenuous* hikes will tax even experienced hikers; and *Strenuous* trails will push the physical limits of the most Herculean hiker.

Following this reference section is a mile-by-mile breakdown of the trail using landmarks, trail junctions, and gradient changes. Note that most trail signs in the park have distances posted in kilometers; an easy rule of thumb is that five km is roughly equal to three miles.

The trail breakdown is followed by a detailed interpretive description of the trail, including geologic and ecological features, fishing opportunities, campsites, an elevation chart, and other important information. Photographs have been included to give the reader a visual preview of some of the prominent features along the trail.

Planning Your Trip

Only backpackers with backcountry permits may camp and build fires in designated areas on the trail system. These permits are free-of-charge and are available on a first-come, first-served basis from all visitor centers and many ranger stations. For backpacks in popular areas, it is wise to get your permits a day in advance of the start of your trip. Permits are not required for day trips. Hikers planning to do off-trail climbing or mountaineering are advised to register at any ranger station or visitor center before setting off. Fishermen should be aware of special regulations concerning catch limits and closed water in the park. No formal license or permit is required.

The key to a quality hiking experience is good planning. Hikers who underestimate the distance or time required in completing a hike may find themselves hiking in the dark, a dangerous proposition at best. An experienced hiker traveling at a fast clip without rest stops can generally make three miles per hour on any terrain, and perhaps more if the distance is all downhill. Novices and out-of-shape hikers generally have a maximum speed of 2.5 miles per hour. Note that these rates do not include stops for rest and refreshment, which add tremendously to the hiker's enjoyment and

Looking up Canyon Creek valley.

appreciation of the surroundings. Eight miles a day is a good goal for travelers new to backpacking, while old hands can generally cover at least twelve miles comfortably. To fully enjoy your hike, travel below top speed, focusing more attention on the surrounding natural beauty and less on the exercise of hiking itself.

A FEW WORDS OF CAUTION

Weather. Weather patterns in the mountains of Glacier National Park may change frequently and without warning. Cold temperatures can occur even during the height of summer, and nighttime temperatures routinely dip into the forties and even thirties on clear nights. Thunderstorms may change cloudless days into a drenching misery, so appropriate rain gear should be carried by all hikers. Ponchos are generally sufficient for day hikes, but backpackers should carry full rain suits, as water from wet vegetation will quickly soak travelers who rely solely on ponchos for protection. Through June and starting again in late August, snowfall is a distinct possibility in the high country, and overnight backpackers should carry clothing and gear with this possibility in mind. Detailed short range forecasts are available at visitor centers and are usually reliable.

Grizzly Bears. Grizzly bears are natural residents of Glacier National Park, and you will be passing through their territory during the course of day hikes and backpacks. By exercising precautions and treating the bears with respect, the hiker can minimize the chances of confrontation or harmful encounters with these wild and beautiful creatures. First of all, give bears a wide berth,

4

as the bear will perceive a direct approach as a threat. Many a photographer has met his end while trying to get just a little closer for that perfect shot. Females with cubs and bears in the vicinity of a kill are particularly sensitive to intrusions by humans.

In camp, cook all food in designated cooking sites at least one hundred yards from your tent site, as the odors produced by cooking may attract scavenging bears. *Always* hang all food on cache poles and wires provided at each campground. Bring a rope at least thirty feet long for this purpose. Hanging your pack not only prevents bear encounters, it also protects your pack from rodents which chew at packstraps for their salt. In areas of dense brush along trails, it may be necessary to announce your presence to bears. Bearbells may be worn for this purpose; clapping and shouting at appropriate times works just as well.

Remember that a bear will try to avoid contact with humans, so if you meet a bear along the trail, the odds are good that he will turn and flee. In the event of a human-bear confrontation, the best course of action is to talk in a firm, unexcited voice to the bear while waving your arms slowly and backing away. Do not attempt to run away from the bear, as this action may cause the bear to identify you as prey and give chase. With a top speed of forty miles per hour, a grizzly can certainly catch a running person if it has the inclination. Climbing a tree is a means of escape if an appropriate tree is nearby and one has sufficient time to do so (which is usually not the case). Playing dead— curling into a ball face-down and covering the neck and stomach—should only be used as a last resort after the bear has decided to attack. This action may save the victim from mortal wounds. It is easier by far to avoid a bear encounter than to get out of one.

Water Supplies. The pristine streams and lakes of Glacier National Park are quite refreshing, but may contain a microorganism called *Giardia lamblia*, which causes severe diarrhea and dehydration in humans. The microorganism is spread through the feces of mammals, especially beavers which inhabit many low-elevation stream systems. The water can be rendered safe by boiling it for at least one minute or by passing it through a filter system with a mesh no larger than two microns. Iodine tablets and other purification additives are not considered completely effective against *Giardia*. Any surface water supply is a potential source of this organism, and hikers that drink from lakes and streams assume the risk of contracting the painful symptoms.

THE NORTH FORK

The North Fork of the Flathead River runs through a broad, forested valley bounded to the west by the Whitefish Range and on the east by the craggy Livingston Range. Trails generally begin among low ridges and wind into the high country through deep, forested valleys. The climate here reflects the maritime influence of storm fronts from the Pacific, and as a result the North Fork country gets quite a bit of percipitation over the course of a year; most of which falls in the wintertime as snow. The vegetation of the valley floor is dominated by lodgepole pines, which are dependent on periodic fires to maintain a competitive edge over more shade-tolerant species. The *serotinous* cones of lodgepoles are covered with resin that melts and allows the cone to release seeds only in the presence of heat provided by forest fires. The seeds then fall on fertile soil in openings created by the fire, where they germinate and thrive in the direct sunlight. This valley was occasionally used by the Salish-speaking natives of the inland Northwest for hunting and gathering purposes on their way to the plains buffalo hunting grounds.

Wildlife in this part of the park reflects the boreal nature of the region, with elk and white-tailed deer being plentiful, and signs of taiga species such as the lynx and the fisher are occasionally seen among the thick stands of lodgepole pine at lower elevations. The only active wolf pack in the western U.S. makes the North Fork valley its home, and hikers that see tracks or hear the howl of this endangered animal can consider themselves truly fortunate. Bird watchers will find the large glacial lakes of this area good places to see ospreys, bald eagles, and common loons.

The North Fork valley can be accessed via the Inside North Fork road (Glacier Route 7), which runs along the river, inside the park boundary. There are auto campgrounds at Quartz and Logging creeks along this improved gravel road, as well as campgrounds at the foot of Bowman and Kintla lakes. An alternate route into the North Fork area is the Polebridge Road, which can be accessed from the terminus of the Camas Road or from the town of Columbia Falls, and runs sixteen miles north to the settlement of Polebridge. This road is heavily traveled by logging trucks and is frequently in rough condition. Just north of this quaint community, a new two-lane bridge crosses the river to link up with Glacier Route Seven. Polebridge is an authentic frontier community, serving a handful of homesteads and ranches on the west bank of the river. This "town" boasts a mercantile store which sells gas and groceries and the Northern Lights Saloon, which serves meals and libations to the weary traveler in an atmosphere of down-home hospitality.

Most of the hikes in the North Fork stick to the lower elevations, and the closed canopy of the forest makes for limited views along the trail. Burns and lakes provide occasional vistas, while the forest itself abounds with wild berries in the late summer. Lakes and streams typically harbor native west-slope cutthroat trout; rainbow trout were also introduced in some areas. In general, the lakes provide much better fishing than the streams, because the streams are very pure and contain few nutrients to sustain a productive food web. Check the park fishing regulations for closures and catch limits before you set out.

Looking west across Upper Kintla Lake.

TRAIL 1 _BOULDER PASS_

General description: A backpack from Kintla L. to Upper Kintla campground, 11.6 mi. (18.5 km); from Kintla Lake to Boulder Pass, 17.7 mi. (28.5 km); or from Kintla Lake to Goat Haunt R.S., 31.4 mi. (50.5 km)
Elevation gain: 3,470 ft.
Elevation loss: 2,510 ft.
Maximum elevation: 7,478 ft.
Difficulty: Moderately strenuous (east to west); strenuous (west to east)
Topo maps: Kintla Lake, Kintla Peak, Mt. Carter, Porcupine Ridge
Finding the trailhead: Drive north on Glacier Route 7 to its northern terminus at Kintla campground. The trail begins at the northeast corner of the campground, near the lakeshore.

0.0   Trail sign. Trail follows shore of Kintla Lake.
3.6   Junction with connecting trail to Kishenehn R.S. Keep right for Boulder Pass trail.
6.3   Kintla Lake campground. Trail leaves Kintla Lake, moderate uphill to Upper Kintla Lake.
9.0   Foot of Upper Kintla Lake. Trail follows shore of Upper Kintla Lake.
11.6   Upper Kintla campground. Trail crosses Kintla Creek and ascends steeply to Boulder Pass campground.
17.2   Boulder Pass campground.
17.7   Boulder Pass. Junction campground is .1 mile to the left. Stay to right for Boulder Pass trail, which descends moderately steeply into Hole in the Wall.
21.2   Junction with trail into Hole in the Wall campground (.5 mi.)—stay left for Brown Pass.
22.8   Brown Pass. Junction with trail to Bowman Lake. Stay left for trail to Goat Haunt R.S., which descends moderately steeply to Olson Creek.
24.9   Hawksbill campground. Trail gradually descends through Olson Creek valley.
25.1   Junction with spur trail to Lake Francis campground.
27.9   Lake Janet campground.
30.9   Junction with Waterton Lake trail. Stay right for Goat Haunt R.S.; turn left to Waterton township (8.7 mi.).
31.1   Suspension bridge over Waterton River.
31.2   Junction with Rainbow Falls trail. Stay left for Goat Haunt.
31.4   Goat Haunt R.S.

The trail: The Boulder Pass trail provides access to some of the most rugged and beautiful high country areas in Glacier Park. High elevations between Boulder and Brown passes lead to high snow accumulations and late snow melt, making this trail impassable early in the season. This trail may be entered and exited via three trailheads: Kintla Lake, Goat Haunt Ranger Station, and Bowman Lake (see separate listing). Any combination of hiking experiences, from day hikes to extended expeditions, are available to hikers on this trail.

    The trail begins at Kintla Lake, which is set in a forested valley between

TRAIL 1 and 4 *BOULDER PASS, BOWMAN LAKE-BROWN PASS*

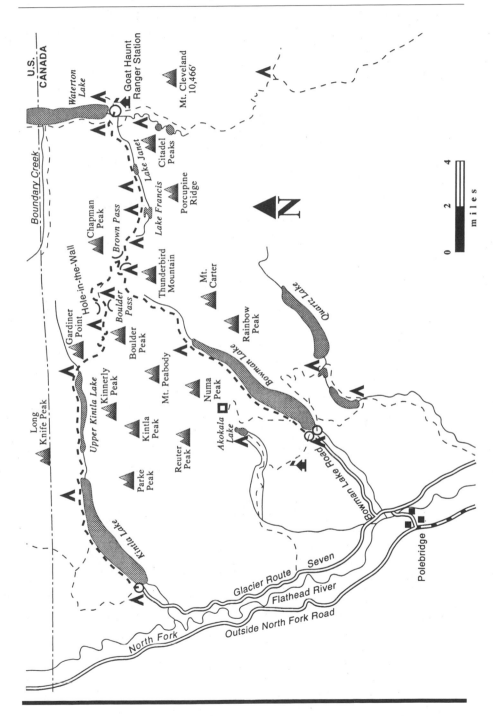

tree-clad hills. As the trail winds around the north lakeshore, watch for signs of mule deer and mountain lions which inhabit the dense forest. Approximately 3.5 miles from the campground, a primitive connecting trail from Starvation Creek joins the Boulder Pass trail from the north. The Boulder Pass trail continues to follow the lakeshore for another three miles to Kintla Lake (head) campground, a heavily used area on the lakeshore.

Shortly after the campground, at the head of the lake, the trail passes the Kintla Lake patrol cabin, where the trail leaves the lakeshore to begin a gentle ascent to Upper Kintla Lake. The trail passes up wooded benches, just out of sight of the cascades of Kintla Creek. Occasional avalanche chutes from Long Knife Peak provide vistas of Parke Peak and the Harris Glacier across the valley. The trail reaches the foot of Upper Kintla Lake some 2.5 miles beyond the patrol cabin. The cockscomb peak at the head of the lake is Gardner Point. The trail follows the north shore of the lake, providing views of Kinnerly Peak across the valley. After 2.5 miles, the trail reaches a spur trail to the campground at the head of the lake, which is beautifully situated among stands of fir and spruce.

Leaving the lakeshore and campground behind, the trail crosses Kintla Creek and begins a steep ascent along the west slope of Gardner Point. There are many switchbacks through scattered stands of spruce and open jungles of cow parsnip, a favorite springtime food for grizzlies, before the trail emerges into alpine parkland at the head of the small valley. All along this section of the trail are views of Kintla and Kinnerly peaks to the west, and the Agassiz Glacier at their feet. Looking back toward Upper Kintla Lake, Long Knife Peak can be seen, marking the boundary between Canada and the U.S. The trail then reverses its direction, climbing northward to the Boulder Pass Campground. Just below the pass, the trail passes through stands of young alpine larch, an uncommon tree which exists here near the southern extreme of its range.

From the west end of Boulder Pass, the trail winds for several miles through a high, glacier-carved valley, across moraines left by retreating glaciers. Pyramid-shaped piles of rock called cairns mark the location of the trail so that it can be found in times of deep snow. At the east end of the pass, the trail branches into two parts. The more northerly path is now a goat path, which ascends the terminal moraine of Boulder Glacier and winds upward for a mile to a lookout point, high above the Bowman Valley. This lookout affords the most spectacular views of Thunderbird Mountain and many of the high peaks of the Livingston and Lewis ranges.

The more southerly path descends onto a rocky shelf occupied by several tarns and continues its decent around the curve of the Hole in the Wall, a perfectly formed hanging cirque which sits some 1,800 feet above the floor of the Bowman Valley. There are deep snowdrifts along this section, usually until August. When the trail reaches the eastern edge of the Hole in the Wall, a spur trail descends to the floor of the cirque, where a beautiful alpine campground is located among meadows of wildflowers and subalpine firs. This campground is frequented by several pestiferous mule deer, which should not be fed for any reason.

After passing Hole in the Wall, the trail continues its gentle descent to Brown Pass, a low saddle at the base of Thunderbird Mountain. Huckleberries grow in great profusion along this section of trail and provide a free food source for hikers and animals alike when they ripen in early August. At the

Thunderbird Mountain from Boulder Pass overlook.

pass is the junction with the Bowman Lake trail. A short jaunt of .3 mile down this trail brings the hiker to the Brown Pass campground, a pleasant area set among windblown firs. Looking eastward from Brown Pass, the jagged spur ridge shaped like a wolf's lower jaw is Citadel Peaks, and the massive peak behind it is Mt. Cleveland, at 10,466 ft. the highest point in the park. After Brown Pass, the Boulder Pass tail descends steeply beneath the Thunderbird Glacier to a tarn at the head of Olson Creek valley. A steep snowdrift extends down to the edge of the water in spring, and several early-season hikers have slid down the drift to receive an icy and unplanned bath. The pond itself is set among dense willows and may harbor an occasional moose.

Once the trail reaches the valley floor, it begins a long, slow descent to the Waterton Valley. The trail passes through a fairly open section to Hawksbill Campground, a small area situated below a clifflike spur ridge scraped sheer on both sides by glaciers. The trail continues eastward through open forest to the junction with a spur trail to Lake Francis campground, which lies on the shore of a beautiful lake beneath rocky cliffs. The lake

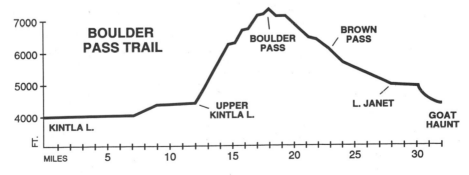

is noted for its mosquitoes and fine fishing for rainbow trout. The trail continues to the Lake Janet campground, which is located on the bank of Olson Creek, some distance from its namesake lake. Grizzly bears are frequently spotted in the avalanche paths on the ridge above this campground.

The trail continues down the Olson Creek valley, past shallow, and sometimes mucky, Lake Janet, and into a forest of Douglas-firs. An occasional opening in the canopy provides a backward look at glacier-clad Porcupine Ridge, as well as views of Citadel Peaks and Mt. Cleveland ahead. Finally, the trail makes a brief descent to the floor of the Waterton Valley and meets the Waterton Lake trail. To reach Goat Haunt, the trail turns south and east, crossing the Waterton River via a suspension bridge and then turning north to the ranger station complex.

TRAIL 2 *AKOKALA LAKE*

General description: A day hike or short backpack from Bowman campground to Akokala Lake, 5.8 mi. (9.5 km)
Elevation gain: 1,105 ft.
Elevation loss: 400 ft.
Maximum elevation: 5,135 ft.
Difficulty: Moderate
Topo maps: Quartz Ridge, Kintla Pk.
Finding the trailhead: Take Glacier Route 7 north to Bowman Lake Road turnoff, just north of Polebridge. Take Bowman Lake Road east to terminus at Bowman campground. Trail departs from north side of campground, away from the lakeshore.

0.0 Trail sign. Trail ascends Numa Ridge, then descends steeply to Akokala Creek.
3.6 Junction with Akokala Creek trail. Stay right for Akokala Lake.
5.8 Akokala Lake campground.

The trail: This trail provides a pleasant hike across wooded ridges and valleys to a low-elevation lake surrounded by precipitous peaks. The trail leaves Bowman campground, climbing through dense forest and swamplands to the ridgeline of Numa Ridge. Along the crest of the ridge, openings were created by the 1988 North Fork fire, which allowed enough sunlight to reach the forest floor for beargrass and other wildflowers to proliferate.

AKOKALA LAKE

The trail descends steeply, once again entering dense "doghair" lodgepole stands, until it reaches Akokala Creek. The trail turns eastward, following the rushing course of the stream upward through more burned areas. The trail rises gently and then levels out shortly before reaching the marshy shores of Akokala Lake and its campsite at the outlet.

TRAIL 2 and 3 *AKOKALA LAKE, NUMA RIDGE L.O.*

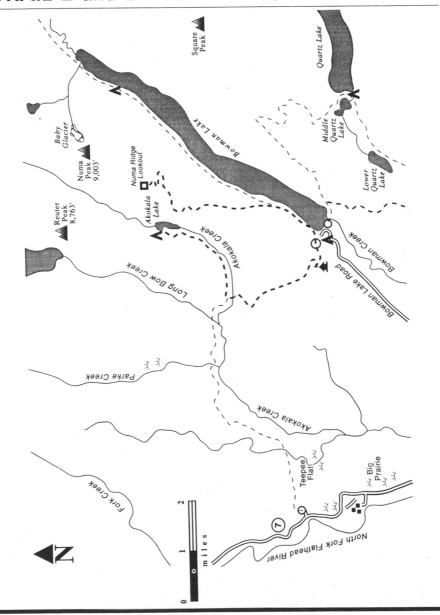

A short trip through dense underbrush lands the hiker on the south shore of the lake, with its magnificent view of the peaks beyond. Reuter Peak and the south ridge of Kintla Peak form the northern rim of the valley, while the pointed summit of Mt. Peabody can be seen at the valley's head. Numa Peak rises steeply to the east, overshadowing the south shore of the lake. Akokala Lake is frequently murky and is not known for its fishing.

TRAIL 3 *NUMA RIDGE LOOKOUT* see p. 13 for map

General description: A day hike from Bowman campground to Numa Ridge Lookout, 5.6 mi. (9 km)
Elevation gain: 2,930 ft.
Maximum elevation: 6,960 ft.
Difficulty: Moderate
Topo maps: Quartz Ridge, Kintla Pk.
Finding the trailhead: Bowman Lake trailhead, Bowman campground (see Bowman Lake-Brown Pass for details).

0.0   Trail sign. Trail follows shore of Bowman Lake.
0.7   Junction with Numa Ridge L.O. trail. Stay left for Numa Ridge L.O. Trail ascends south face of Numa Ridge, then follows ridgeline to lookout.
5.6   Numa Ridge Lookout.

The trail: Numa Ridge Lookout is one of the easiest lookouts to reach in the park. The trail climbs 3,000 feet over the course of five miles, passing up the forested flanks of Numa Ridge to a swampy saddle, which is good habitat for northern bog lemmings. The trail climbs out of the trees onto an open, grassy swale for the last .25 mile. Upon reaching the lookout, which lies on the west face of Numa Ridge, the hiker will find spectacular views of Square Peak, Rainbow Peak, and Mt. Carter across Bowman Lake, plus sweeping vistas of the Whitefish Range across the forested North Fork. Akokala Lake and Reuter Peak lie to the north of the lookout. Bring water.

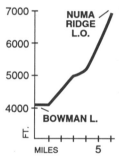

NUMA RIDGE L.O.

Bowman Lake and Mt. Carter. Photo by Michael S. Sample.

TRAIL 4 BOWMAN LAKE-BROWN PASS see p. 9 for map

General description: A backpack from Bowman Lake to Brown Pass, 13.8 mi. (22 km)
Elevation gain: 2,200 ft.
Maximum elevation: 6,255 ft.
Difficulty: Moderately strenuous
Topo maps: Quartz Ridge, Kintla Peak, Mt. Carter
Finding the trailhead: Follow Glacier Route 7 north to junction with Bowman Lake Road, just north of Polebridge. Take Bowman Lake Road (a narrow, but graded gravel road) to terminus at Bowman campground. Trail departs from northeast corner of campground, near the lakeshore.

0.0 Trail sign. Trail follows shore of Bowman Lake.
0.7 Junction with Numa Lookout trail. Stay right for Brown Pass.
7.1 Bowman Lake (head) campground. Trail ascends gently, crossing Pocket and Bowman creeks, then ascends steeply to Brown Pass.
13.6 Brown Pass Campground
13.8 Brown Pass. Junction with Boulder Pass trail.

The trail: The Bowman Lake trail may be used as a backpack in itself, or in conjunction with the Boulder Pass trail for extended trips. The trail winds past Bowman Lake before ascending a U-shaped valley carved by a glacier between rugged peaks. Ultimately, the trail climbs to Brown Pass, where views of peaks and glaciers can be seen in all directions.

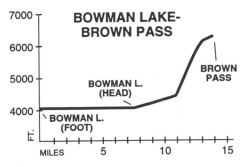

The trail follows the northwestern shore of Bowman Lake for seven miles of gentle up and down hiking to a backcountry campsite near the head of the lake, popular with hikers and boaters alike. The lake is prime osprey and bald eagle habitat, and the lake is frequently closed to boating, fishing, and hiking above the upper campground to protect the nest sites of eagles. Views across the lake include Square Peak, Rainbow Peak, and Mt. Carter.

Brown Pass Option. The trail leaves the lakeshore after the upper campground, climbing gently through forest and marsh. The valley is populated with wary herds of elk. The bugling vocalizations of bull elk announcing their presence to females can sometimes be heard echoing off of the cliff walls in late August and early September. About three miles beyond the campground, the trail crosses Pocket Creek and Bowman Creek in short order, and then continues for another half mile to the base of Brown Pass.

At this point, the trail begins a steep ascent around the north slope of Thunderbird Mountain. Clearings in the forest provide views of Hole in the Wall Falls across the valley and Boulder Peak high above. Halfway to the pass, the forest opens into open brushy meadows with babbling brooks and small

Bowman Lake. Photo by Matt Culter.

waterfalls. Shortly before reaching the pass, the trail passes through the Brown Pass campground, set among dense stands of subalpine fir. When the trail reaches the pass, one can see the serrated ridge of the Citadel Peaks and the massive bulk of Mt. Cleveland by looking east, down the Olson Creek valley.

TRAIL 5 *QUARTZ LAKES LOOP*

General description: A day hike or short backpack from Bowman Campground to Quartz Lake, 6.2 mi. (10 km.); round trip, 12.8 mi. (20.5 km.)
Elevation gain to Upper Quartz Lake: 1,470 ft.
Elevation loss to Upper Quartz Lake: 1,100 ft.
Maximum elevation: 5,500 ft.
Difficulty: Moderate
Topo map: Quartz Ridge
Finding the trailhead: Trail departs from the southeast corner of the Bowman campground, at the backcountry parking area. See Bowman Lake-Brown Pass for further details.

0.0 Trail sign. Trail crosses Bowman Creek and ascends gradually along the shore of Bowman Lake.
0.4 Junction with Quartz Lakes trail. Stay left for Quartz Lake; turn right for Lower Quartz Lake. Trail to the left ascends gradually to ridgeline, then descends moderately steeply to Quartz Lake.
6.2 Quartz Lake campground. Trail to Lower Quartz Lake departs from the

southwest corner of the campground. Trail follows the south shore of Middle Quartz Lake, then descends to Lower Quartz and follows the lakeshore to the outlet stream.

9.3 Lower Quartz campground. Loop trail crosses the outlet stream to the north. Trail to the southwest follows Quartz Creek to Glacier Rt. 7 (6.8 mi.). Trail crosses Cerulean Ridge.

12.4 Trail junction with trunk trail to Bowman campground. Turn left to return to starting point.

The trail: The Quartz Lakes Loop begins and ends at the Bowman Lake auto campground. It passes over the crest of Cerulean Ridge to drop into the Quartz Creek valley at Quartz Lake, then turns southwest for three miles along the valley floor before climbing back over the ridge to its starting point. The loop makes for a pleasant day hike, and there are several backcountry camping areas for hikers looking for an overnight experience. The loop can also be accessed via a seven-mile trail that runs up Quartz Creek from the Inside North Fork Road.

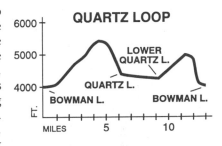

QUARTZ LOOP

TRAIL 5 *QUARTZ LAKES LOOP*

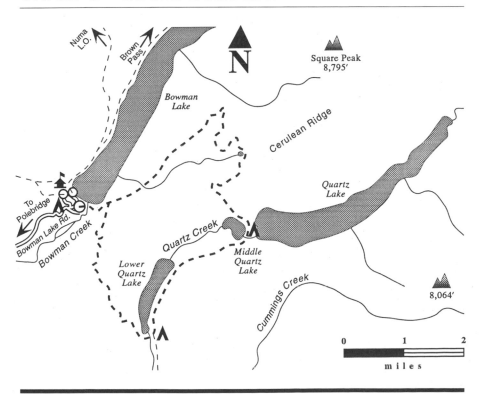

After leaving the Bowman Lake campground, the loop begins as a trunk trail that crosses Bowman Creek at the foot of the lake and winds around the south shore to rise for .4 mile to a fork. The easier route is the left fork, which allows the hiker to hike the loop in a clockwise direction. This fork rises gently for about 2.5 miles to the crest of Cerulean Ridge, and then crosses the ridge crest into the Quartz Creek drainage. The trail dips into an area burned in the 1988 North Fork fire, where fireweed and grasses have colonized and begun the succession back to forest. The opening of the forest canopy allows views of the rugged outlying mountains of the Livingston Range, including Logging Mountain in the foreground and the taller, more jagged Vulture Peak behind it. The trail descends to a campground at the foot of Quartz Lake, which supports a good population of rainbow and cutthroat trout.

The trail exits this campground from its west side and runs southwest, passing the south shore of shallow Middle Quartz Lake. The trail continues through open forest to the southwest for about a mile before reaching the head of Lower Quartz Lake, which it follows to its foot. At the campground set on both sides of the outlet, the trail forks. The Quartz Creek trail continues to follow the south bank of the creek to the Inside North Fork Road, while the loop trail crosses the outlet via a trail bridge and turns northward. From this point, the trail climbs through the burn to crest the ridge, at which point it reenters the forest for a rather steep descent back to the trunk trail, .4 mile from the trailhead.

TRAIL 6 *LOGGING LAKE*

General description: A day hike or backpack from Glacier Route 7 to Logging Lake, 4.4 mi. (7 km); or Glacier Route 7 to Grace Lake, 12.8 mi. (20.5 km)
Elevation gain: 477 ft.
Maximum elevation: 3,930 ft.
Difficulty: Easy
Topo maps: Demers Ridge, Vulture Pk.
Finding the trailhead: Logging Creek campground, twenty miles north of the Camas Road junction.

0.0	Trail sign
4.4	Logging Lake. Trail follows the north shore of the lake.
4.9	Junction with Logging patrol cabin trail (.2 mi.). Stay left.
5.0	Junction with Lower Logging campground trail (.2 mi.). Stay left.
9.8	Adair campground.
11.4	Head of Logging Lake.
12.8	Grace Lake campground.

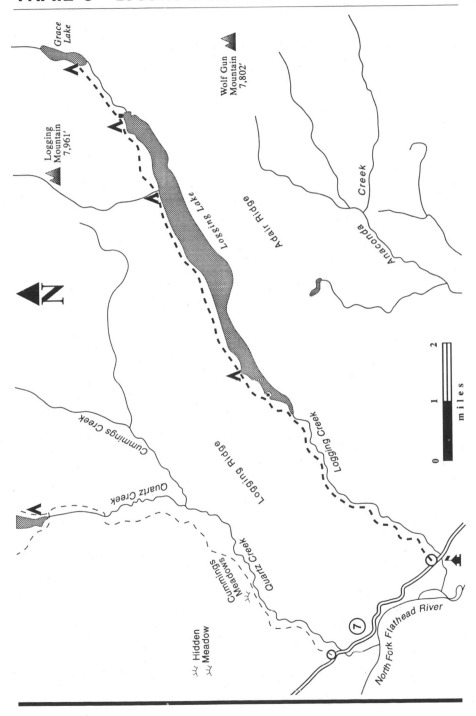

Grace Lake

Wolf Gun Mountain 7,802'

Logging Mountain 7,961'

Logging Lake

Adair Ridge

Anaconda Creek

N

miles
0   1   2

Cummings Creek

Quartz Creek

Logging Creek

Logging Ridge

Cummings Meadows

Quartz Creek

Hidden Meadow

North Fork Flathead River

7

The trail: The Logging Lake trail follows the course of Logging Creek from the North Fork lowlands to its headwaters in the Livingston Range. The trail starts off with a short climb to the top of a densely wooded plateau, and then proceeds along the rim of a shallow canyon. As is typical of North Fork trails, this trail provides an easy

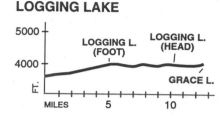

hike through gentle terrain that is dominated by old growth conifers with dense underbrush. Occasionally, the trail ventures near the rim of a small canyon, offering a brief glimpse of Logging Creek below. In accordance with its gentle terrain and mature forests, the trail offers no views of the glacier-carved peaks until it reaches Logging Lake.

The first campground along the trail is about half a mile east of the lake's outlet, on the north shore. This campground, situated on a beautiful little bay, affords the first view of the lake and the peaks that rise at its eastern end. Mt. Geduhn and Anaconda Mountain rise at the head of the valley. There is no free-flowing water source near this campground.

Four miles further along the trail is the next campsite at Adair Creek. The view here is less spectacular but the creek provides a supply of running water to the campsite. From this point, it is approximately 1.5 miles to the head of the lake. The head of Logging Lake is currently closed to fishing and most other human activity because it is a nesting area for bald eagles. A few fortunate hikers may be treated to the sights and sounds of adult eagles teaching their young to fly, fish, and hunt for food. If you are one of the lucky ones, take care to remain hidden, as eagles are easily disturbed by the presence of humans.

Looking northeast across Logging Lake from the campground at the foot. Photo by Matt Cutler.

Grace Lake Option. Grace Lake is about a mile and a half further up the trail from the head of Logging Lake, a total of twelve miles from the trailhead. Grace Lake is reported to provide the finest fishing in the park, as it supports a large population of healthy west-slope cutthroat trout. This lake is nestled among the peaks of the Livingston Range. Because thick timber surrounds most of the lake, fly casting is a difficult proposition. However, a short bushwhack to the head of the lake provides access to a talus slope with ample casting room for the fisherman. The campsite at Grace Lake is seldom visited and provides solitude for the hardy souls who reach it.

Wildlife is abundant along the entire length of the trail. Deer, squirrels, and even mountain lions inhabit the forested valley, and the call of the loon is frequently heard on Logging Lake. *—Matt Cutler*

CONNECTING TRAILS

Kishenehn Creek trails. A network of primitive trails runs north from the Inside North Fork road to Kishenehn Creek patrol cabin and beyond to the Canadian border via Kishenehn Creek or the North Fork of the Flathead River. An access trail runs from the Kishenehn Creek trail across Starvation Creek and Ridge to Kintla Lake. The Kishenehn complex is used primarily for administrative and fire suppression purposes. The trail from the foot of Kintla Lake to Kishenehn Creek has been abandoned, as has the trail up Starvation Creek. Similarly, the trail from Round Prairie to the foot of Kintla Lake has been abandoned.

An administrative trail up **Akokala Creek** exists between the North Fork Road and the West Lakes trail (running from Bowman to Akokala Lakes). This trail receives a low level of maintenance and is difficult to find in places.

A secondary trail runs along **Quartz Creek** some seven miles from the Quartz Creek Campground to Lower Quartz Lake. This trail is moderately popular with horse parties.

Dutch Creek complex. The complex of trails between Logging Creek and Dutch Creek has been abandoned. The Dutch Lake trail is covered with blown-down lodgepole pines that have been killed by pine bark beetles. The fallen trees are generally cut out each year.

THE LAKE McDONALD AREA

Lake McDonald, near the west entrance of Glacier, is the largest body of water in the park. It is ten miles long and has a maximum depth of 472 feet. The lake's bed was carved out by a huge glacier that filled the entire valley, leaving a characteristic U-shaped basin. Lake McDonald was once pretty fair fishing for native cutthroat trout, but the introduction of lake trout wiped out the cutthroat population, and the lake now provides very poor fishing. At the foot of the lake lie the low foothills of the Apgar Range and Belton Hills, while the snow-capped peaks of the Continental Divide loom to the east of the lake's head. The country is characterized by low, east-west running ridges rising in the east to rugged peaks. The entire area is densely covered with forests, grading from cedars, birches, and larches at the lower elevations to Douglas-firs and lodgepole pines higher up.

West Glacier is the western gateway to the park and serves as the trailhead and rafting hub for the western side of the park. A wide variety of tourist services are offered at West Glacier, Apgar Village, and Lake McDonald Lodge, including guided horse trips, gas, restaurants, and lodging. Belton Chalets, Inc., runs the Sperry Chalets, which can only be reached via foot or horseback along the Gunsight Pass trail (see St. Mary section). Reservations should be made far in advance for all lodging accommodations. Major car campgrounds are located at Apgar and Avalanche Creek, and these tend to be crowded and noisy. A quieter tents-only campground is located on Sprague Creek near Lake McDonald Lodge. The Going-to-the-Sun Highway is closed to bicyclists from 11:00 a.m. to 4:00 p.m. over most of its length due to the heavy car traffic on this narrow road during midday.

Looking across Lake McDonald at Mt. Vaught (far left). Photo by Matt Culter.

Goats at Gunsight Pass.

Hikes in the Lake McDonald area tend to pass through heavy forest, with little opportunity for sweeping views until treeline is reached. Wildlife viewing opportunities are somewhat limited due to the dense vegetation, but mountain lions, deer, and elk all inhabit the forested foothills around Lake McDonald. The high country is home to mountain goats as well as smaller denizens of the talus slopes, including marmots and ground squirrels. Loons and bald eagles are occasionally seen on the glacial lakes that dot the area.

TRAIL 7 *TROUT LAKE*

General description: A day hike or backpack from North McDonald Road trailhead to Trout Lake, 3.5 mi. (5.5 km.); North McDonald Road to Arrow Lake campground, 6.9 mi. (11 km.); North McDonald Road trailhead to Camas Lake, 10.5 mi. (17 km.); or Glacier Rt. 7 to Camas Lake, 13.9 mi. (22.5 km)
Elevation gain to Camas Lake: 3,150 ft.
Elevation loss to Camas Lake: 1,230 ft.
Maximum elevation: 5,353 ft.
Difficulty: Moderately strenuous
Topo maps: Camas Ridge East, Mt. Cannon
Finding the trailhead: Take the Going-to-the-Sun Road .5 mile east of Lake McDonald Lodge to the North Lake McDonald Road, which enters from the north. Turn north, and drive across McDonald Creek and around the east side of Lake McDonald. The pavement will end shortly after the McDonald Creek Bridge; continue past the Lake McDonald Ranger Station approximately .5 mile

TRAIL 7 *TROUT LAKE*

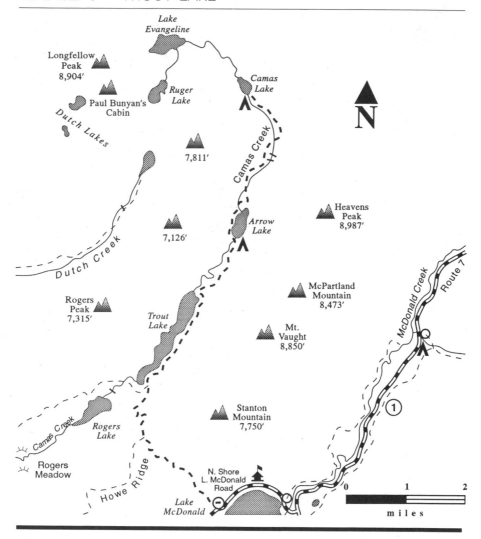

to a marked trailhead sign with a wide spot for parking. The Trout Lake trail begins at this wide spot in the road.

0.0 Trail sign. Trail ascends rather steeply to ridgeline.
2.3 Junction with Howe Ridge trail. Stay right for Trout Lake. Trail descends to Trout Lake.
3.5 Junction with Camas Lake trail. Stay right for Trout L.
3.6 Trout Lake (foot). Trail follows lakeshore, then ascends gradually to Arrow Lake.
7.0 Arrow Lake campground. Trail fords Camas Creek to the north shore. Trail follows shore to inlet stream, fords stream, and continues east, up

moderate uphill sections and three additional fords, to Camas Lake.
10.6 Camas Lake campground.

The trail: The lakes of Camas Creek can be reached by a low-maintenance, brushy trail up the creek from the Inside North Fork Road or by using a well-maintained cutoff trail that climbs over Howe Ridge to Trout Lake, a route that is 3.4 miles shorter. Horse parties favor the former route because of its low gradient, while hikers generally prefer the latter. Trout Lake and even Arrow Lake are reasonable day hike destinations from the North McDonald Road, and overnighters can camp at backcountry campsites at Arrow and Camas lakes. Because the trail from Arrow Lake to Camas Lake is quite hard to follow

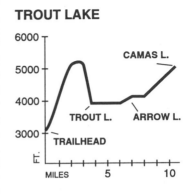

TROUT LAKE

and crosses five major fords, it is recommended only for determined hikers. All waters in the Camas Creek drainage are flyfishing-only; use of spinning tackle is strictly prohibited.

The trail begins on the northeast shore of Lake McDonald, from a dirt road that winds part of the way around the north end of the lake. It climbs quickly to cross a rushing stream, and then ascends the west bank of the stream toward the crest of Howe Ridge. About half way to the top, the trail passes through an opening dominated by beargrass and serviceberry bushes. From here a backward glance reveals Lake McDonald and the peaks to the south. The trail resumes the climb, passing into the woods en route to the wooded saddle where it meets the Howe Ridge trail.

After cresting the ridgeline, the trail descends steeply, switching back across the wooded north slope of Howe Ridge. Shortly before reaching the valley floor, the trail intersects with the Camas Creek trail and turns eastward to the foot of Trout Lake. There is a hitching rail and picnic area at the foot of Trout Lake, and across the lake the arc of Camas Ridge culminates in Rogers Peak. The trail winds along the forested south shore of Trout Lake—occasional avalanche chutes open views to Stanton Mountain and Mt. Vaught—and ascends briefly through Douglas-fir forest, with a huckleberry understory, to Arrow Lake. From this lake, McPartland Mountain and Heavens Peak rise to the east.

Camas Lake Option. The trail to Camas Lake is quite overgrown with head-high cow parsnip by the end of the summer, and crosses no less than five major fords along its 3.6 mile length. The trail begins at the campground at the foot of Arrow Lake and immediately fords the outlet to the far bank of Camas Creek. The trail follows the north shore of the lake to its head, where it crosses the inlet stream before continuing across an overgrown meadow. Here, it may be necessary to look for the blaze orange disks nailed to tree trunks to mark the trail. After leaving the meadow, the trail enters forested bottomland, where it fords Camas Creek again and climbs up its rocky north bank. After surmounting several small hills, the trail emerges into open brushfields, where it descends to the creek and crosses again. These open slopes, overgrown with mountain ash and cow parsnip, dominate the valley as the trail winds around to the northwest toward Camas Lake.

Trout Lake and Heavens Peak.

Upon reaching the foot of the lake, the trail crosses its outlet among wet meadows and willow groves before arriving at the forested campground. The entire Camas valley is prime grizzly bear habitat, so the appropriate precautions should be taken. The view from Camas Lake is somewhat less than spectacular, consisting of the low, brushy ridges immediately surrounding the lake. From this lake, it is possible to bushwhack (in every sense of the word) westward to the lakes at the head of the valley. Lake Evangeline is said to have outstanding fishing, while Ruger Lake sits at the base of stunning Longfellow Peak. A rock formation on an overlooking spur ridge, locally known as Paul Bunyan's Cabin, overshadows Ruger Lake's western shore.

TRAIL 8 *HUCKLEBERRY MOUNTAIN LOOKOUT*

General description: A day hike from Camas Creek Road to Huckleberry L.O., 6.0 mi. (9.5 km)
Elevation gain: 3,403 ft.
Maximum elevation: 6,593 ft.
Difficulty: Moderately strenuous
Topo maps: McGee Meadow, Huckleberry Mtn.
Finding the trailhead: Follow Camas Creek Road west out of Apgar. Trailhead is marked on road, about six miles northwest of Apgar, on the left.

0.0   Trail sign.
6.0   Huckleberry Mountain Lookout.

The trail: This trail begins near McGee Meadows and climbs steeply up the north bank of McGee Creek through forest before emerging above the

TRAIL 8 *HUCKLEBERRY MOUNTAIN LOOKOUT*

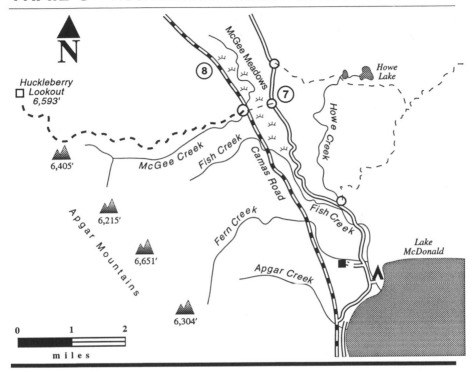

trees. The trail continues to climb until it reaches the ridgeline, and then turns north, following the crest of the Apgar Mountains for 1.5 miles to the lookout.

The slopes below the lookout were burned by a raging wildfire in 1967. The burn site has been colonized by dense stands of lodgepole pines locally known as "doghair." The cones of lodgepoles are *serotinous*, which means that they remain sealed until the high temperatures of fires melt the seal around the cone, allowing them to open and release the seeds. A few huge larch trees survived

HUCKLEBERRY MTN.

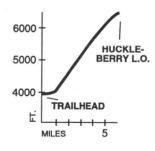

the fire by virtue of their thick bark, which peels away from the trunk as it burns, thus protecting the living cambium under the bark from fire damage. The seedlings of both larch and lodgepoles require the open sunlight provided by burned areas to germinate and are known as "fire-adapted" species.

From the lookout, the uninterrupted forests of the North Fork valley stretch away to the foot of the snow-capped Livingston Range, which dominates the eastern skyline. —*Matt Cutler*

TRAIL 9 *APGAR LOOKOUT*

General description: A half-day hike from Rubideau Road to Apgar Lookout, 2.8 mi. (4.5 km)

Elevation gain: 1,835 ft.

Maximum elevation: 5,236 ft.

Difficulty: Moderate

Topo map: McGee Meadow

Finding the trailhead: Take the Apgar horse corral road, halfway between West Glacier and Apgar. Follow this road to a Y-intersection. Keep left, following the sign to Quarter-Circle Bridge. Cross the bridge and follow the easily passable (road signs to the contrary) road for approximately one mile. Turn right at the first opportunity, following the trailhead sign, and follow this road .5 mile to the Apgar Lookout trailhead.

0.0   Trail sign. Trail follows old dirt road.
0.8   Trail leaves dirt road, begins ascent of Apgar Mountain.
2.8   Apgar Lookout.

TRAIL 9 *APGAR LOOKOUT*

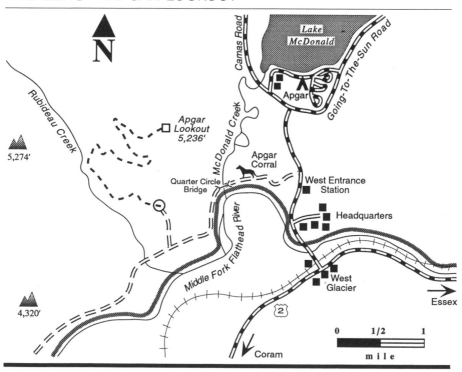

The trail: This trail provides a short, yet challenging hike that ends with an unusual view of Lake McDonald and the Livingston Range beyond. The trail starts out as a primitive road, winding across the benchland below Apgar Mountain. Eventually, the road ends and the trail begins a moderately steep ascent, switching back across the south face of the hill and affording an occasional glimpse through openings in the trees of the mountain ranges south of the park. The Flathead Range rises to the southeast, dominated by the snow-capped peak of Great Northern Mountain, the highest peak in the Great Bear Wilderness. Looking further west, the Swan Range trails away to the south. In berry season, thimbleberries along the trail provide snacks for hungry hikers, and there are small patches of huckleberry bushes near the lookout. There are no permanent streams on Apgar Mountain, so canteens are highly recommended for this trail.

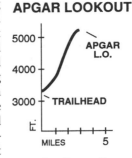

APGAR LOOKOUT

Once the lookout is reached, the view stretching away to the east reveals the entire length of the Livingston Range, with Lake McDonald prominently nestled among its foothills. The Belton Hills rise steeply at the foot of the lake. Mounts Vaught and Brown are the prominent peaks flanking the upper end of McDonald Lake, and the Garden Wall can be seen at the head of the valley.

TRAIL 10 *LINCOLN LAKE*

General description: A day hike or backpack from Lincoln Lake trailhead to Lincoln Lake, 8.0 mi. (13 km)
Elevation gain: 2,250 ft.
Elevation loss: 800 ft.
Maximum elevation: 4,900 ft.
Difficulty: Moderately strenuous
Topo maps: L. McDonald West, L. McDonald East
Finding the trailhead: Lincoln Lake trailhead, marked as such by a trail sign on the Going-to-the-Sun Highway, approximately 1.5 miles west of Lake McDonald Lodge.

0.0 Trail sign. Trail climbs steeply to ridgeline.
1.7 Junction with Snyder Ridge trail. Stay straight for Lincoln Lake. Trail descends moderately to Lincoln Creek.
4.4 Junction with Lincoln Creek trail. Turn left for Lincoln Lake. Trail ascends gently to Lincoln Lake.
8.0 Lincoln Lake campground.

The trail: Lincoln Lake is a low-elevation cirque lake that sits at the foot of 1,344-foot Beaver Chief Falls. It can be reached by an arduous hike over Snyder Ridge from the shores of Lake McDonald or by taking a longer, poorly maintained route up Lincoln Creek from the South Boundary trail. Views along both routes are minimal until the lake is reached.

The trail begins at a marked trailhead on the Going-to-the-Sun Road and

TRAIL 10 *LINCOLN LAKE*

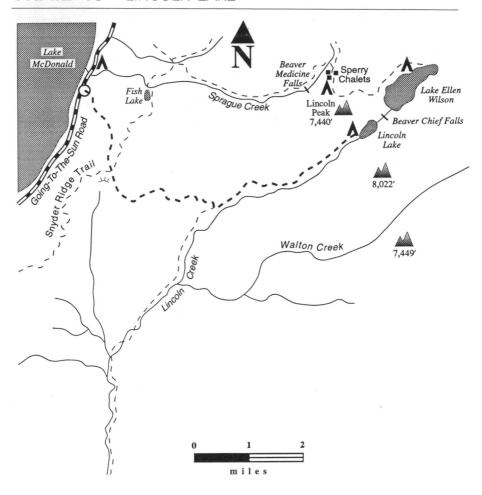

LINCOLN LAKE

wastes no time in climbing steeply and steadily up forested slopes to the crest of Snyder Ridge. The mossy understory of this forest is home to the pale purple lady slipper orchid, which can be seen in bloom in early summer. At the crest of the ridge, the trail crosses the Snyder Ridge fire trail and continues to rise gently on wooded benchland. Winding around the south face of a hillside, openings in the trees provide glimpses of the snow-capped Flathead Range to the south of the park. Beargrass dominates the understory of the pine forest on dry sites. This plant blooms on a three- to five-year cycle, and local populations of the plant tend to be synchronized, so that on favorable

Lincoln Lake and Beaver Chief Falls.

years, the profusion of beargrass inflorescences brightens the entire forest. The trail continues to dip and rise as it passes through tiny dales before descending steadily to Lincoln Creek.

Upon reaching the valley floor, the trail enters a series of wet meadows in the forest, on which deer and other animals may be seen in early morning and late evening. The trail running up the creek valley is boggy after snowmelt and becomes quite overgrown with cow parsnip and thimbleberry late in the summer. Brief glimpses of the sheer walls of the valley can be had through the trees along the route to the lake, which is prime black bear habitat.

Upon reaching the lakeshore, the forest opens up to reveal spectacular cliffs on three sides of the lake, with Beaver Chief Falls coursing down the valley's headwall. Above this cirque is a higher cirque containing Lake Ellen Wilson, which was carved out by glaciers after the lower cirque had already been formed. When two or more cirques are superimposed on each other, the resulting geologic feature is called a *compound cirque*. The campground sits at the foot of the lake, near its shallow outlet. The lake is fair fishing for pan-sized cutthroats and larger brook trout.

TRAIL 11 *FISH LAKE*

General description: A half-day hike from Snyder Creek trailhead to Fish Lake, 2.4 mi. (4 km)
Elevation gain: 1,000 ft.
Maximum elevation: 4,150 ft.
Difficulty: Moderate
Topo map: L. McDonald East
Finding the trailhead: Snyder Creek trailhead, across the Going-to-the-Sun Road from Lake McDonald Lodge.

0.0   Unnamed trailhead.
0.1   Trail sign beyond stables. Stay right for Fish Lake. Trail ascends moderately, following Snyder Creek.
1.7   Junction with Mt. Brown Lookout trail. Stay right for Fish Lake.
1.8   Trail junction with Snyder Lakes trail. Stay right for Fish Lake. Trail crosses Snyder Creek.
1.9   Junction with Snyder Ridge trail. Turn right for Fish L. Trail turns west along benches of Snyder Ridge.
2.4   Fish Lake.

TRAILS 11, 12, and 13   *FISH LAKE, MT. BROWN L.O., SNYDER LAKES*

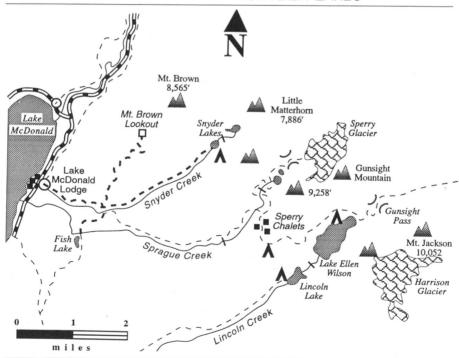

The trail: Fish Lake provides a pleasant hike across wooded ridges to a quiet, reedy lake nestled among tall conifers. The trail follows Snyder Creek for two miles, climbing steadily through dense forests, with cedars, hemlocks, and larches of the lower elevations giving way to white pines and Douglas-firs. The trail crosses Snyder Creek at mile two, and the Fish Creek trail branches off to the west immediately on the west bank of the creek. From this point, the trail ascends slightly to crest wooded benches, winding through a mossy forest to Fish Lake. The lake itself is set in a small forested pocket in Snyder Ridge, from which only the surrounding forest can be seen. Loons are commonly sighted on this small lake, which makes an ideal picnic spot. The Snyder Ridge trail (poorly maintained) continues west from Fish Lake for eight miles, eventually returning to the Going-to-the-Sun Road shortly above the foot of Lake McDonald.

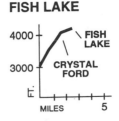

FISH LAKE

TRAIL 12 *MT. BROWN LOOKOUT*

General description: A day hike from Snyder Cr. trailhead to Mt. Brown L.O., 5.4 mi. (8.5 km)
Elevation gain: 4,305 ft.
Maximum elevation: 7,487 ft.
Difficulty: Strenuous
Topo maps: L. McDonald East, Mt. Cannon
Finding the trailhead: Snyder Creek trailhead, marked with a trailhead sign on the Going-to-the-Sun Highway, immediately across from the Lake McDonald Lodge coffee shop.

0.0 Unnamed trailhead.
0.1 Trail sign beyond stables. Stay right for Mt. Brown L.O. Trail climbs moderately, following Snyder Creek.
1.7 Junction with Mt. Brown Lookout trail. Turn left for Mt. Brown Lookout. Trail switchbacks steeply up the flanks of Mt. Brown.
5.8 Mt. Brown Lookout.

The trail: The trail to the Mt. Brown Lookout is one of the steepest and most grueling trails in the park. It climbs to a fire lookout on a false summit of the peak, affording an unusual view of Lake McDonald and the mountains in the vicinity of Sperry Glacier. The trail begins in the cedar and larch lowlands near Lake McDonald and climbs up Snyder Creek into a forest dominated by Douglas-fir. At mile 1.7, the lookout trail climbs steeply to the north, beginning a steady, leg-burning ascent up switchbacks toward the summit. As the trail climbs upward, it passes through subalpine firs and huckleberry patches higher up before emerging onto an open ridgeline shortly before the lookout. The Park Service has

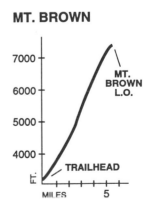

MT. BROWN

placed a booklet on the history of the fire lookout on the catwalk outside, as well as a log book for hikers to record their own impressions. To the northeast along the ridgeline lies the Little Matterhorn, while the large mountain further south is Edwards Mountain. The summit of Mt. Brown lies one mile to the north and can only be reached by a technical ascent.

TRAIL 13 SNYDER LAKES see p. 32 for map

General description: A day hike or short backpack from Snyder Creek trailhead to Snyder Lake, 4.4 mi. (7 km)
Elevation gain: 2,047 ft.
Maximum elevation: 5,230 ft.
Difficulty: Moderate
Topo maps: L. McDonald West, L. McDonald East, Mt. Cannon
Finding the trailhead: Snyder Creek trailhead, a marked trailhead on the Going-to-the-Sun Road, immediately across from the Lake McDonald Lodge coffee shop.

0.0 Unmarked trailhead.
0.1 Trail sign, beyond stables. Stay right for Snyder Lakes. Trail ascends moderately, following Snyder Creek.
1.7 Junction with Mt. Brown Lookout trail. Stay right for Snyder Lakes.
1.8 Junction with Snyder Lake trail. Turn left for Snyder Lakes. Trail ascends gently to Snyder Lake.
4.4 Snyder Lake.

The trail: This trail provides a nice medium-distance day hike or short backpack from Lake McDonald Lodge. From the trailhead, the hiker moves through tall cedars into a higher forest of Douglas-fir and larch. The trail follows Snyder Creek eastward. At mile 1.8, the Snyder Lake trail turns northeast, following Snyder Creek, while the main trail crosses the creek and continues southeastward to Sprague Creek.

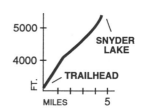

The Snyder Lake trail winds upward gently, through boggy openings, mountain ash thickets, and stands of Douglas-fir and subalpine fir. Early in the year, this section of the trail can be quite muddy; waterproof boots are a must. After 2.5 miles, the trail reaches a campground at the outlet of Snyder Lake. This lake is inhabited by cutthroat trout. Upper Snyder Lake is accessible by bushwhacking up the talus slope on the west side of the cliff at the head of the lake, and then scrambling up one of the narrow gullies that pierces the cliff at this point. The lakes are set beneath the soaring cliffs of Mt. Brown, the Little Matterhorn, and Edwards Mountain. The cliffs are discolored by patches of green and black crustose lichens, fascinating organisms that incorporate separate fungus and algae organisms into one functional unit. On the far side of the Little Matterhorn lies the Avalanche Basin and Sperry Glacier high above it.

TRAIL 14 *AVALANCHE LAKE*

General description: A half-day hike from Avalanche Creek trailhead to Avalanche Lake, 2.9 mi. (4.5 km)
Elevation gain: 505 ft.
Maximum elevation: 3,905 ft.
Difficulty: Easy
Topo map: Mt. Cannon
Finding the trailhead: Trail of the Cedars trailhead, across the Going-to-the-Sun Highway from Avalanche campground.

0.0   Trail of the Cedars boardwalk trail.
0.1   Trail leaves boardwalk and crosses Avalanche Creek. Junction with Avalanche Creek trail. Turn left for Avalanche Lake.
2.1   Avalanche Lake (foot).
2.9   Avalanche Lake (head).

The trail: The Avalanche Lake trail is one of the most popular hikes in the park, due to its gentle grade and spectacular destination. Hikers seeking solitude should go elsewhere, as throngs of bearbell-bedecked tourists are a given at the height of the season.

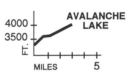

AVALANCHE LAKE

The trail begins at the Trail of the Cedars, a handicapped-accessible boardwalk that winds between the boles of huge cedars and cottonwoods to Avalanche Gorge. The gorge was formed by the force of the stream cutting down through argillite beds, forming fantastic bowls and chutes in the rock. The spray from small waterfalls provides the moisture needed to sustain the profusion of mosses that drape the rocks surrounding the gorge. Water ouzels are commonly seen flying along the watercourse and occasionally diving into the churning water, to emerge unharmed and execute "pushups" on the rocks along the stream.

The trail follows the west rim of the gorge, through stands of western hemlock, identified by its drooping topmost leader. This tree is limited to areas of high rainfall, as are the cedars below. The trail winds upward through the forest, following the course of Avalanche Creek. Across the valley to the northeast, the valley of Hidden Creek joins the Avalanche Creek valley. The trail continues upward through sparse timber and dense underbrush until it reaches the foot of the lake.

Avalanche Lake is rimmed by steep cliffs on three sides. Bearhat Mountain forms the east wall of the valley, while the west wall is formed by Mount Brown. To the south, at the head of the valley, numerous waterfalls cascade downward from the hanging cirque valley formed by Sperry Glacier, which cannot be seen from the lake.

The trail continues around the western shore of the lake to its inlet, where fair fishing for native west-slope cutthroats can be had (possession limit is two). Looking north from the head of the lake, Heavens Peak is beautifully framed by the walls of the Avalanche Creek valley.

TRAIL 14 *AVALANCHE LAKE*

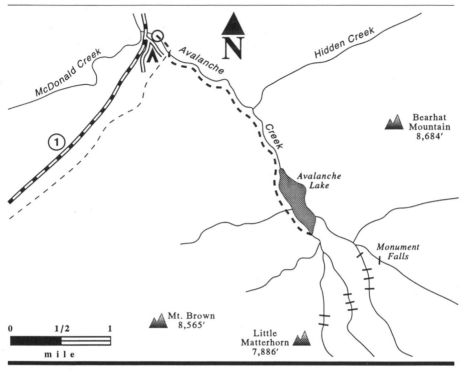

ADDITIONAL TRAILS

The **Camas Creek trail** is a lightly maintained trail that runs for seven miles through meadows of tall forbs and grasses and Douglas-fir woodlands to Trout Lake. Although the trail is quite brushy in places, it is the favored route for horse parties accessing the Camas Creek Valley.

The **Howe Lake trail** begins at mile 7.3 of the North Fork Road, and winds two miles to marshy Howe Lake, where a lucky hiker might encounter both moose and beaver. The trail continues 1.8 miles to connect with the Howe Ridge trail. The Howe Ridge trail is a secondary fire access trail that follows a wooded ridgeline eastward from the Howe Creek bridge to its junction with the Trout Lake trail, above Kelly Camp trailhead.

There is an unmaintained trail that runs from mile 3.4 of the Camas Road up the south bank of **Fern Creek** for three miles, through a mixed forest of larch and Douglas-fir. The trail is difficult to find in places and therefore not recommended for hiking.

McDonald Creek has a gentle trail following its course on each side from the east end of the lake. The west bank trail runs from the automobile bridge over upper McDonald Creek along the creek for 3.4 miles, passing above Sacred Dancing Cascades in its shallow limestone canyon. Another trail runs from the Snyder Creek trailhead for 5.8 miles to Avalanche campground. The trail passes diminutive Johns Lake as it winds through the woodland, out of sight of creek and road. Until the trail reaches the McDonald Creek horse bridge, it is frequented by horse parties from the Lake McDonald trail guide operation.

Lake McDonald West Shore trail. A trail from the North McDonald Road runs for two miles through wooded country to a backcountry campground known as Kelly Camp. This campground is also available to non-motorized boat users on the lake. From the campground, the trail continues to follow the lakeshore in a southwesterly direction, ultimately reaching the Camas Road near Fish Creek.

The **Snyder Ridge trail** runs from mile 4.0 of the Going-to-the-Sun Highway, along the wooded ridge past a junction with the Lincoln Lake trail, to Fish Lake and beyond to Snyder Creek. The trail is well maintained only between the Lincoln Lake trail and Snyder Creek.

A poorly maintained trail runs from the south boundary trail up **Lincoln Creek** to a junction with the Lincoln Lake trail. This trail is very brushy and has no views to recommend it.

THE HIGHLINE AND THE WATERTON LAKE VICINITY

The Highline trail runs along the Continental Divide for almost twenty miles from Logan Pass to Fifty Mountain campground where it joins the Waterton Valley trail in its descent to Goat Haunt Ranger Station on Waterton Lake. For most of its length, the trail runs through alpine meadows, with snowy crags rising on all sides. Wildflower enthusiasts will find the meadows along the trail bursting with a profusion of blossoms throughout the summer. The high, open slopes above the trail provide the finest wildlife viewing opportunities in the park. Bighorn sheep and mountain goats skirt the bases of towering cliffs, while marmots and pikas scramble around on boulderfields. Colonies of Columbia ground squirrels in the open meadows provide hours of entertainment for travelers who watch the cavorting antics of these social rodents.

Further north, the Waterton River valley boasts the best moose habitat in the park. Trails from Waterton Lake connect with short day hiking opportunities as well as longer hikes in Waterton National Park in Canada. The North Fork area can be reached via the Boulder Pass trail, providing options for extended backpacks.

The Highline itself is closed to horse traffic from Logan Pass to Granite Park, but a trail along the crest of Flattop Mountain allows horse parties access to the Fifty Mountain area. There are major visitor centers at the north end of the Highline. A number of trails connect the Highline with the North Fork, Belly River, and Many Glacier areas, making the Highline a central component of many extended backcountry expeditions. With this in mind, the

Mts. Oberlin, Clements, and Cannon.

campground at Granite Park is generally reserved during July and August for backpackers with extended itineraries. Granite Park Chalet is a privately run concession that provides limited meals and lodging for travelers; reservations are often required well in advance.

TRAIL 15 *HIDDEN LAKE*

General description: A half-day hike from Logan Pass to Hidden Lake overlook, 1.5 mi. (3.5 km), and from Logan Pass to Hidden Lake, 3.0 mi. (5 km)
Elevation gain: 550 ft.
Elevation loss: 675 ft.
Maximum elevation: 7,050 ft.
Difficulty: Moderate
Topo maps: Logan Pass, Mt. Cannon
Finding the trailhead: Trail begins immediately behind Logan Pass Visitor Center.

0.0 Trail sign.
1.4 Hidden Lake Pass.
1.5 Hidden Lake overlook. Trail descends fairly steeply to Hidden Lake.
3.0 Hidden Lake.

The trail: The trail to Hidden Lake provides one of the quickest access routes to the high country in Glacier Park. It starts as a boardwalk which climbs moderately through fields of wildflowers to Hidden Lake Pass, in the shadow

Bearhat Mountain and Hidden Lake.

TRAIL 15 *HIDDEN LAKE*

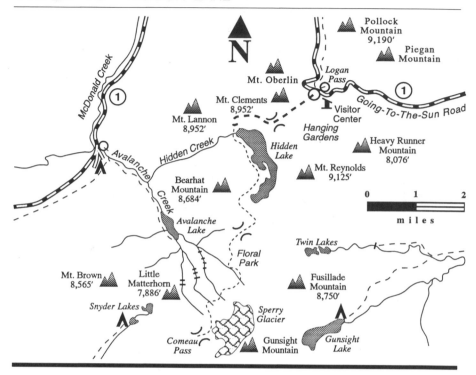

of Mt. Clements. From the pass, Mt. Reynolds dominates the southern skyline, while Bearhat Mountain rises on the far side of islet-strewn Hidden Lake. A third of a mile further is an overlook point, from which the trail descends almost 700 ft. to the north shore of the lake, which is reputed to contain large but wary cutthroat trout. A mountaineer's route begins at the south end of the lake, skirting the base of the cliffs

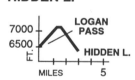

along the Continental Divide and then dropping into Floral Park and crossing below the Sperry Glacier to Comeau Pass.

TRAIL 16 *THE GARDEN WALL*

General description: A day hike or extended backpack from Logan Pass to Granite Park Chalet, 7.6 mi. (12 km), or from Logan Pass to the Loop, 11.6 mi. (18.5 km)
Elevation gain: 830 ft.
Elevation loss: 3,026 ft.
Maximum elevation: 7,280 ft.
Difficulty: Easy

Topo maps: Logan Pass, Many Glacier, Ahern Pass
Finding the trailhead: Trail begins at Logan Pass, across the highway from the visitor center. Exit point is "the Loop," the large hairpin turn on Going-to-the-Sun Road, about seven miles west of the pass.

0.0	Trail sign.
3.4	Saddle behind Haystack Butte.
6.8	Junction with Grinnell Glacier overlook trail (.8 mi., maximum elevation 7,600 ft., moderately strenuous). Stay left for Granite Park.
7.6	Granite Park Chalet. Junction with trails leading to Swiftcurrent Pass (.9 mi., moderate), Swiftcurrent Lookout (2.3 mi., moderately strenuous), and the northern Highline trail. Turn left for the Loop.
7.8	Junction with Granite Park campground trail. Stay left for the Loop.
11.4	Junction with Loop cutoff trail. Turn left for the Loop.
11.6	Trail exit at the Loop.

The trail: The Garden Wall section of the Highline trail is one of the most popular hikes in the park, owing to its spectacular vistas, excellent wildlife viewing opportunities, and low level of difficulty. The trail follows the west face of the Continental Divide, maintaining a relatively constant elevation, to Granite Park Chalet, a privately run concession that offers rooms (booked far in advance) and meals (reservations suggested). The campground at Granite Park is limited to backpackers on extended trips for most of the season. From Granite Park, the trail leads down to the Going-to-the-Sun Road, terminating at "the Loop," the northernmost hairpin turn on the highway. A spur trail also leads from this trail to "Packers Roost," further down the mountainside.

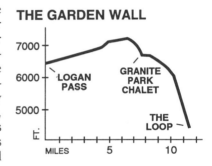

The Highline trail crosses excellent habitat for many types of wildlife, and the open subalpine meadows of the Garden Wall allow easy viewing of wild creatures in their natural environments. Columbia ground squirrels abound in the alpine tundra areas, and hoary marmots and pikas are frequently seen among the boulders of talus slopes below cliff faces. Look for mountain goats and bighorn sheep near the bases of the cliffs and among stands of fir. Raptors are commonly seen soaring on thermals high above the alpine meadows, hunting for rodents. The campground at Granite Park is frequented by mule deer, many with impressive racks that remain in velvet throughout the summer. Please do not feed the wildlife in the interest of keeping it wild.

The trail begins at Logan Pass, winding through the twisted forms of subalpine firs and Engelmann spruce. Strong prevailing winds in wintertime blow ice particles that tear the branches from the windward side of the trees, creating a flaglike appearance. In areas of especially high wind, all branches exposed above the snowline may be pruned by windblown ice, creating a low, matlike growth form called *krummholtz* in adult spruce and firs.

After several hundred yards, the trail winds around a sheer cliff face, high above the valley below. The trail continues northward through open stands of fir, following in the shadow of the Garden Wall. This land form was created

TRAIL 16 *THE GARDEN WALL*

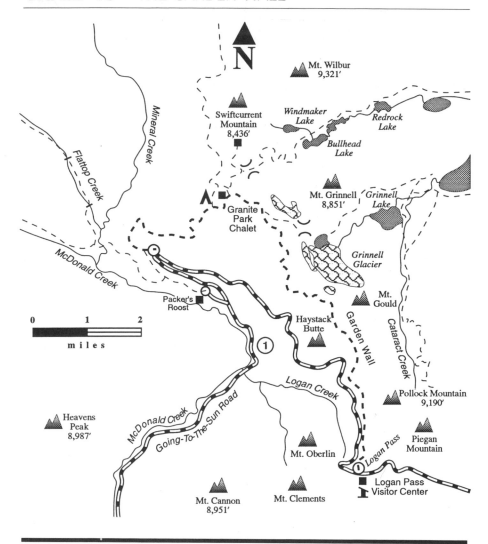

by the action of glaciers moving down valleys on both sides of a mountain mass. The resulting knife-edge ridge is called an *arete*. Across the valley, Mounts Oberlin, Clements, and Cannon cradle a high hanging basin formed by glaciers, from which Bird Woman Falls cascades hundreds of feet to the valley floor. The trail emerges into alpine tundra spangled with wildflowers, past gushing rills with their staircase cascades. The trail climbs gently to pass behind Haystack Butte, a rounded promontory jutting into the Logan Creek valley, which makes an ideal lunch spot. Golden-mantled ground squirrels, identified by the alternating stripes of black and blond on their backs, inhabit the slopes around Haystack Butte.

Bighorn sheep in Glacier National Park. Photo by Michael S. Sample

As the trail winds northward beyond Haystack Butte, it crosses barren, rocky slopes interspersed with mountain meadows. At mile 6.8, the trail to the Grinnell Glacier overlook enters from the east. This trail is .8 mile long and fairly steep, running upward to a high notch in the Garden Wall which overlooks Grinnell Glacier on the east side of the divide. From the terminus of the spur trail, a goat trail winds around to the right, passing along the eastern face of the Garden Wall to a narrow notch which affords a superior view of the glacier.

The Highline trail continues northward for less than one mile, reaching a trail junction at Granite Park Chalet. Views from the Chalet include Heavens Peak immediately across the valley, as well as other snow-capped peaks of the Livingston Range trailing away to the north.

From Granite Park Chalet, trails branch off in many directions, offering interesting day trips and backpacking possibilities. To the west, the connecting trail descends past the campground trail junction to switch back down to the Loop, the northern terminus for most hikers. The eastern fork becomes the northern continuation of the Highline trail, discussed in the following trail description, from which routes to Swiftcurrent Pass and Lookout branch after .2 mile. Swiftcurrent Lookout provides a sweeping view of the Swiftcurrent drainage, as well as views to the west, after a challenging climb rising 1,000 feet over 2.3 miles. Swiftcurrent Pass is a low saddle with no particularly scenic views until the hiker is descending, which provides trail access to the Many Glacier area.

TRAIL 17 *THE NORTHERN HIGHLINE*

General description: An extended backpack from Granite Park to Fifty Mountain campground, 11.9 mi. (19 km)
Elevation gain: 1,910 ft.
Elevation loss: 1,780 ft.
Maximum elevation: 7,440 ft.
Difficulty: Moderate
Topo map: Ahern Pass
Finding the trailhead: Granite Park Chalet, reached via Logan Pass or the Loop (see The Garden Wall), or Fifty Mountain campground, reached via Goat Haunt (see Waterton Valley trail).

0.0   Trail sign, Granite Park Chalet.
0.2   Junction with Swiftcurrent Pass trail. Stay left for the Northern Highline.
0.5   Junction with Granite Park campground trail. Stay right for the Northern Highline.
4.5   Junction with Ahern Pass trail (0.4 mi., easy). Stay left for Fifty Mountain.
6.5   Trail reaches its lowest elevation as it crosses Cattle Queen Creek.
10.9   Junction with Sue Lake overlook trail (0.4 mi., maximum elevation 7,700 ft., strenuous). Stay left for Fifty Mountain.
11.9   Fifty Mountain campground.

The trail: The northern section of the Highline trail is accessible only to hikers on extended trips of more than one night. It runs from Granite Park Chalet to Fifty Mountain campground, connecting the Garden Wall trail and the Many Glacier complex with trails out of Goat Haunt on Waterton Lake. The trail stays high in the subalpine country throughout its entire length,

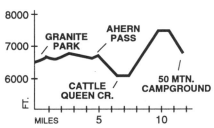

NORTHERN HIGHLINE

and sublime views can be had at any point along the trail.

The trail begins by passing around the east side of the chalet and quickly winds around a meadowy spur ridge and out of sight. Meadows along the trail contain glacier lilies, mountain asters, shooting stars, and Indian paintbrushes at different times of the summer. To the west, the peaks of the Livingston Range are constant companions to the hiker as the trail runs to the north. To the west lies Heavens Peak, while Longfellow Peak is the large mountain further to the north and behind it. Several miles out from the chalet, the trail rounds a rocky knob and turns eastward briefly, hugging the cliff wall. A persistent snowdrift in this area makes early season travel on this section hazardous if not impossible. The rocky basin beyond is prime habitat for mountain goats and hoary marmots, who graze together in the meadows below the cliff walls.

As the trail reaches the north end of the basin, another trail cuts off to the

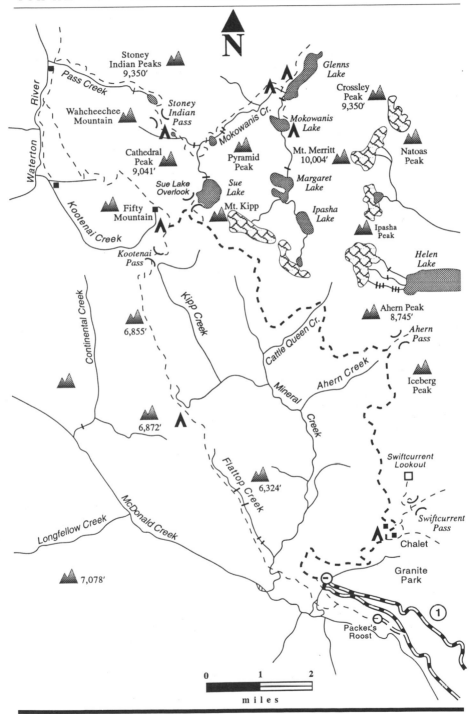

N

Stoney
Indian Peaks
9,350'

Pass Creek

River

Waterton

Wahcheechee
Mountain

*Stoney
Indian
Pass*

Glenns
Lake

Crossley
Peak
9,350'

Mokowanis Cr.

*Mokowanis
Lake*

Mt. Merritt
10,004'

Natoas
Peak

Cathedral
Peak
9,041'

Pyramid
Peak

*Sue Lake
Overlook*

*Sue
Lake*

Mt. Kipp

*Margaret
Lake*

*Ipasha
Lake*

Ipasha
Peak

*Helen
Lake*

Kootenai Creek

Fifty
Mountain

*Kootenai
Pass*

Ahern Peak
8,745'

*Ahern
Pass*

6,855'

Kipp Creek

Continental Creek

Cattle Queen Cr.

Ahern Creek

Iceberg
Peak

Mineral

6,872'

Creek

*Swiftcurrent
Lookout*

Flattop Creek

6,324'

*Swiftcurrent
Pass*

McDonald Creek

Longfellow Creek

Chalet

Granite
Park

7,078'

Packer's
Roost

1

```
0        1        2
m i l e s
```

Looking back along the Highline Trail to Bird Woman Falls. Photo by Matt Cutler.

east, traveling .4 mile to the low saddle of Ahern Pass. From the vicinity of the pass, the Ahern Glacier can be seen clinging to the southeast face of Ipasha Peak, with waterfalls cascading down the cliff face below it into Helen Lake. A mountaineer's route exists to the Iceberg Notch, immediately above the pass; and from the notch seasoned climbers may tempt the fates by passing along a narrow goat trail that hugs the face of Iceberg Peak above several thousand feet of vertical exposure.

Continuing northward from Ahern Pass, the Northern Highline begins a long, gradual descent through open forests of subalpine firs dotted with wildflowers toward Cattle Queen Creek. A hazardous snowslip exists where the trail crosses this creek and may not melt away until late July. Proceed with caution while crossing snowy slopes, as slipping or falling through spells certain injury and may even be fatal. The Cattle Queen valley is rather brushy, with forbidding walls on both sides. From this creek, the trail begins a long and steady ascent, covering almost 2,000 feet in four miles. The trail continues upward beyond the timberline, winding through rocky meadows populated with ground squirrels and songbirds.

A mile before reaching the campground, the trail reaches its highest point as it passes over a rocky saddle in a scree slope wasteland. The snow-capped peaks of the Livingston Mountains stretch away as far as the eye can see to the west and south, while Mt. Kipp overlooks the trail to the east. The rocky ridge with serpentine snowfields on its face is Trapper Peak, with pyramid-shaped Mt. Geduhn behind it to the south. The horn peak to the south of Geduhn is Anaconda Peak.

Just north of this saddle, a spur trail ascends steeply to a notch that overlooks Sue Lake and the glacier-clad summits of the Mokowanis River valley. The main trail descends into the forest fringe that occupies the edge of the high shelf below, where it enters Fifty Mountain campground. This campground is a favorite haunt of mule deer, which will often approach quite near to visitors who remain still. Please do not feed the wildlife, as feeding encourages the animals to scavenge for human refuse instead of foraging for their natural foods. Trails from the campground descend to the west to Flattop Mountain and to the north to Goat Haunt Ranger Station.

TRAIL 18 *WATERTON VALLEY*

General description: A half-day hike or short backpack from Goat Haunt R.S. to Kootenai Lakes, 2.8 mi. (4.5 km), or a backpack from Goat Haunt to Fifty Mtn. campground, 10.5 mi. (17 km)
Elevation gain to Fifty Mtn.: 2,480 ft.
Maximum elevation: 7,000 ft.
Difficulty: Easy (to Kootenai Lakes); strenuous (to Fifty Mtn.)
Topo maps: Porcupine Ridge, Mt. Geduhn, Ahern Pass
Finding the trailhead: Goat Haunt Ranger Station, reached by ferry from Waterton (Alta.) townsite, or by trail along the western shore of Waterton Lake. The trailhead is located next to the stables, south of the ranger station.

0.0   Trail sign. Trail follows the Waterton Valley floor.
2.5   Junction with Kootenai Lakes trail (0.3 mi.). Stay left for Fifty Mountain.

TRAIL 18 *WATERTON VALLEY*

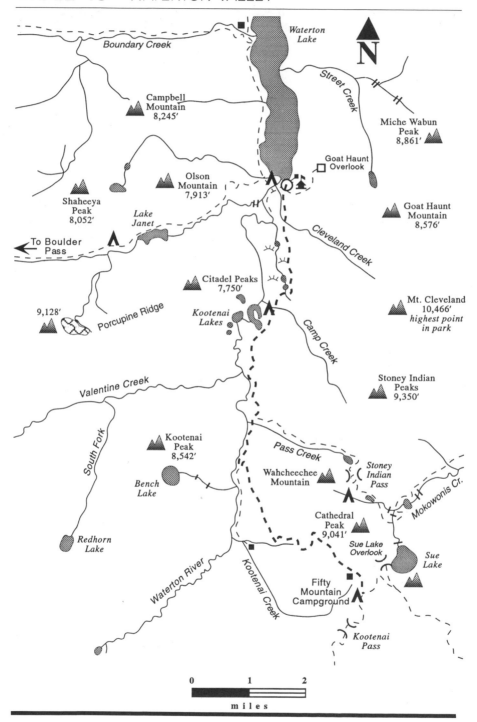

Waterton Lake

Boundary Creek

Street Creek

N

Campbell
Mountain
8,245'

Miche Wabun
Peak
8,861'

Goat Haunt
Overlook

Olson
Mountain
7,913'

Goat Haunt
Mountain
8,576'

Shaheeya
Peak
8,052'

*Lake
Janet*

Cleveland Creek

To Boulder
Pass

Citadel Peaks
7,750'

Mt. Cleveland
10,466'
*highest point
in park*

9,128'

Porcupine Ridge

*Kootenai
Lakes*

Camp Creek

Valentine Creek

Stoney Indian
Peaks
9,350'

South Fork

Kootenai
Peak
8,542'

Pass Creek

*Stoney
Indian
Pass*

*Bench
Lake*

Wahcheechee
Mountain

*Redhorn
Lake*

Mokowonis Cr.

Cathedral
Peak
9,041'

*Sue Lake
Overlook*

*Sue
Lake*

Waterton River

Kootenai Creek

Fifty
Mountain
Campground

*Kootenai
Pass*

0   1   2

m i l e s

48

Moose at Kootenai Lakes.

4.9 Junction with Stoney Indian Pass trail. Stay right for Fifty Mountain.
5.0 Patrol cabin. Trail begins steep ascent along the west slope of the Continental Divide.
10.1 Fifty Mountain saddle.
10.5 Fifty Mountain campground.

The trail: The Waterton Valley trail links Goat Haunt Ranger Station, at the head of Waterton Lake, to the high alpine country of the Highline trail. It offers an easy stroll through the forest on the valley floor to the Stoney Indian Pass junction, then begins a steep, seemingly endless climb across an open, brushy slope to the Fifty Mountain campground. Kootenai Lakes provide a popular day hike destination for fishermen and wild-life viewers from Goat Haunt. The lakes also offer backcountry campsites for a short range, easy backpack.

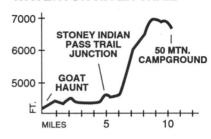

WATERTON RIVER TRAIL

The trailhead for the Waterton Valley trail is behind the stable area in the Goat Haunt Ranger Station complex. After leaving the paved walkways and buildings behind, the trail passes beneath a canopy of large old-growth conifers interrupted by an occasional wet meadow. At mile 2.5 there is a junction with the Kootenai Lakes trail, which runs .3 mile to a campground at the foot of the lower lake. These shallow lakes provide good fishing for large brook trout, and the willows that crowd the shores provide a favored food source for the moose that are frequently seen here. Forested areas provide prime habitat for black bears. The lakes are overlooked to the west by the Citadel Peaks, the rocky spires at the tail end of Porcupine Ridge.

The main valley trail continues southward, rising imperceptibly at first and then climbing into broken hillsides before reaching the junction with the Stoney Indian Pass trail. Near this junction, groves of old-growth spruce grow at the fringes of grassy meadows. About one mile above this junction, the trail begins to climb in earnest, passing high above the rushing torrent of the Waterton River. The trail switchbacks as it climbs out of the forest and onto a hot, west-facing slope covered with cow parsnip and brushy vegetation. For three miles, the trail winds upward, testing the endurance of the most seasoned hiker. The trail passes above a lonely stand of conifers and continues climbing into an alpine parkland below Cathedral Peak, where glacier lilies nod their yellow heads just after snowmelt.

The trail finally reaches its highest point as it passes the ruins of a stone shelter hut, which was never completed, high in an alpine meadow. The view from this point is one of the most spectacular in the park, encompassing the entire Livingston Range and parts of the Lewis Range in the Logan Pass vicinity. From this saddle, it is an easy and short descent into the tree-filled bowl below, where the trail enters the Fifty Mountain campground. This campground is frequented by almost tame mule deer that will try to steal food and sweat-soaked clothing from unwary hikers. Trails leaving the campground run southwest to Flattop Mountain and southeast along the Highline trail to Logan Pass.

Flattop Mountain trail. This trail provides access to the Fifty Mountain area and is frequently used by horse parties. The trail begins at Packer's Roost, a trailhead and old cabin, on a short spur road off the Going-to-the-Sun Highway about twenty-three miles east of West Glacier. The trail follows the floor of the McDonald Creek valley to a crossing of Mineral Creek, where the trail turns north up Flattop Creek. A trail once followed McDonald Creek to West Flattop Mountain, but this trail has been abandoned. The trail climbs to the wooded crest of Flattop Mountain, where occasional openings provide fine views of the surrounding peaks. It is 5.7 miles to the Flattop Mountain campground and 6.3 miles further from this campground to Fifty Mountain campground.

Mineral Creek trail. A low-maintenance status trail runs from the Flattop Mountain trail on the McDonald Creek valley floor up Mineral Creek to an old cabin. The trail is in poor shape and really doesn't access any scenic areas anyway, so there really isn't much reason to venture this way. This was the original trail to Fifty Mountain before the Highline trail was completed from Granite Park in 1932.

Kootenai Creek trail. A low-maintenance trail runs from the Waterton Valley trail southward, following the river to a patrol cabin on Kootenai Creek. The junction is poorly marked and will probably be missed by hikers who aren't looking for it.

Waterton Lake. A trail runs from Goat Haunt around the western shore of Waterton Lake to Waterton township on the Canadian side of the border. There are campsites near the Boulder Pass junction and just north of the Canadian border. The total distance of 6.7 miles can be avoided by taking a tour boat that covers the same route several times a day.

The North Boundary trail. A well-maintained trail runs from the Waterton Lake trail some 5.8 miles up Boundary Creek to the international boundary, where the trail turns north to Summit Lake. There it connects with the scenic Carthew trail which runs west to Cameron Lake and east to Waterton townsite.

Rainbow Falls. A short, well-maintained trail starts with the Waterton Lake trail and runs from Goat Haunt up the east bank of the Waterton River to a series of cascades on the river. The total distance is .7 mile from Goat Haunt, making it a popular day hike for hikers taking the boat tour from Waterton township.

Goat Haunt Overlook. Take the Waterton Valley trail south from Goat Haunt for .1 mile to the Goat Haunt Overlook junction. The overlook trail runs eastward, climbing fairly steeply for one mile on a secondary trail to an overlook high on a spur ridge of Goat Haunt Mountain. From the overlook, Citadel Peaks and the Brown Pass area are visible to the west, and looking north over Waterton Lake, bare peaks stretch away to the horizon.

Goat Haunt Shelters. A short, well-maintained trail runs east for .2 mile around the head of Waterton Lake to the Goat Haunt Shelters, which are located on the hillside above the boat docks.

THE SOUTHERN SECTOR

The entire southwest portion of Glacier National Park is a wild, seldom-visited country that has changed little since pre-Columbian times. Trails tend to favor long-range trips of several days, as the hiker must travel through about seven miles of foothills before reaching the scenic peaks of the spine of the Continental Divide. The distances involved in traveling in the southwest make this area ideal for horse parties. Trails connect this area with the Two Medicine drainage via Cut Bank and Two Medicine passes. This area of the park is the ideal destination for backpackers seeking solitude and a wilderness-oriented experience.

The drainages of Nyack and Coal creeks have been officially designated as a wilderness camping zone. Trails in the zone tend to be primitive, with relatively low maintenance status and many creek fords. Camping is allowed outside designated sites anywhere in the zone by permit (available from the Apgar or St. Mary visitor centers). Developed campsites are also available in the wilderness zone where stock and fires are permitted.

Year-round access to the southwest corner of the park is available via the South Boundary trail from West Glacier in the north and Izaak Walton R.S. in the south. There are also three major foot fords across the Middle Fork of the Flathead River which allow more direct access to this area during the low water months of July and August. Detailed maps of the fords are available at the visitor center at Apgar. The Marias Pass area is accessible via a series of trails that depart from U.S. Highway 2.

Visitor facilities are few and far between on the road between West and East Glacier. Gas and groceries are available near the community of Essex, but the traveler should expect to pay inflated prices here. The historic Izaak

Buffalo Woman Lake on the Nyack Loop.

Walton Inn in Essex was built as a retreat for Great Northern Railway employees and is a center for cross-country skiing activities in the winter and hiking in the summer.

The valley of the Middle Fork is a major wintering ground for the herds of elk that inhabit this area, and ospreys are frequently seen along the river-bank. The valley bottoms of tributary streams provide ideal summer habitat for black bears, and grizzly bears inhabit the more open slopes of the hills above. The southwestern sector receives a fairly high level of winter precipitation, which supports lush forests interrupted by jungles of cow parsnip and thimbleberry. Fishing is prohibited in the streams south of Harrison Creek; Beaver Woman and Buffalo Woman lakes have no fish in them.

TRAIL 19 *HARRISON LAKE*

General description: A day hike (in season) or backpack from U.S. Hwy. 2 to foot of Harrison Lake, 2.9 mi. (4.5 km); from U.S. Hwy. 2 to Harrison L. campground, 4.8 mi. (7.5 km); or from West Glacier to Harrison L. campground, 11.9 mi. (19 km)
Elevation gain: 400 ft.
Maximum elevation: 3,693 ft.
Difficulty: Easy (without ford)
Topo maps: West Glacier, Nyack, L. McDonald East
Finding the trailhead: Ford across Middle Fork of the Flathead River accessible from U.S. Highway 2, 6.5 miles east of West Glacier. For a current map of the ford, please ask at the Apgar Visitor Center. The trail can also be accessed via the South Boundary trail from West Glacier.

0.0 Trail sign, West Glacier. Trail follows Middle Fork of the Flathead eastward.
5.3 Junction with Lincoln Creek trail. Stay right for Harrison Lake.
7.1 Junction with Harrison Lake trail. Turn left for Harrison Lake. Hikers using the Harrison Creek ford enter the trail at this point. Trail climbs gently, following Harrison Creek.
10.0 Foot of Harrison Lake.
11.9 Harrison Lake campground.

The trail: Harrison Lake is a seldom-visited, fairly large lake that sits among forested foothills near West Glacier. It is accessible via ford from U.S. Highway 2 or by hiking the Boundary trail south from West Glacier. The hike ascends a gentle, wooded valley to the foot of the lake, and then follows its western shore. Occasional

HARRISON LAKE

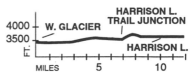

avalanche chutes have made clearings from which Loneman Mountain and Mt. Thompson can be viewed across the lake. The trail reaches its terminus at the head of the lake, which is not particularly noted for its fishing. A trail once climbed toward the head of the valley but is now abandoned.

TRAIL 19 *HARRISON LAKE*

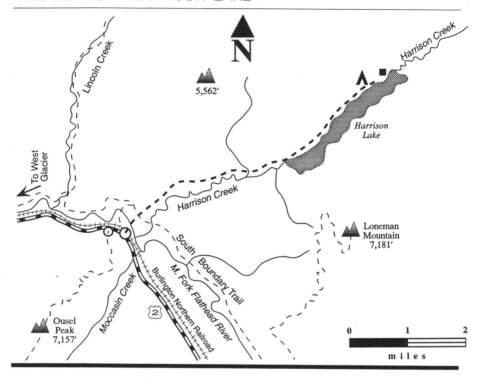

Adventurous hikers may bushwhack their way through dense brush approximately four miles to the head of the valley, where they will be rewarded with spectacular views of waterfalls cascading down from the glaciers poised high on the sides of the surrounding peaks.

TRAIL 20 *LONEMAN LOOKOUT*

General description: A day hike from Nyack Creek ford to Loneman Lookout, 6.5 mi. (10.5 km)
Elevation gain: 3,900 ft.
Maximum elevation: 7,181 ft.
Difficulty: Moderately strenuous
Topo map: Nyack
Finding the trailhead: Nyack Creek ford, accessible from a road off U.S. Highway 2, approximately eleven miles east of West Glacier. Please ask at the Apgar Visitor Center for a detailed map of the ford.

0.0 Nyack trailhead on the north bank of the Middle Fork of the Flathead River.

0.1 Trail sign, beyond old Nyack Ranger Station. Turn left for Loneman Lookout. Trail runs westward, following the Middle Fork.

0.8 Junction with Nyack Creek trail after bridge over Nyack Creek. Stay left for Loneman Lookout.

1.2 Junction with Loneman Lookout trail. Turn right for lookout. Trail ascends fairly steeply to Loneman Lookout.

6.5 Loneman Lookout.

The trail: Loneman Lookout is a seldom-visited, unmanned fire lookout that rises above the old Nyack ranger station. After fording the Middle Fork (ask for conditions), the trail follows the boundary trail north, across Nyack Creek. At mile 1.2, the Loneman Lookout trail leaves the Boundary trail and climbs onto a wooded bench, which it follows for several miles before climbing steeply up the west face of Loneman Mountain. The forest begins to open into grassy meadows halfway to the summit, and the trail makes a complete circuit of the mountain in the last mile of the trail. The summit overlooks Harrison Lake and Walton Mountain to the north, with the peaks of the Great Bear Wilderness looming to the south, crowned with Great Northern Mountain. To the southeast, the fang tooth beyond Threetops Mountain is Mt. St. Nicholas.

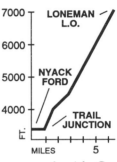

LONEMAN LOOKOUT

TRAIL 20 *LONEMAN LOOKOUT*

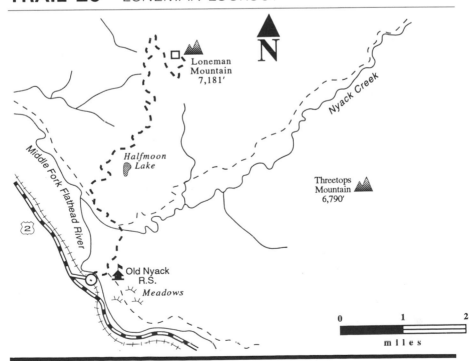

TRAIL 21 *THE NYACK-COAL CREEK LOOP*

General description: A backpack from Nyack Creek ford to Coal Creek ford, 34 mi. (54.5 km), or Round trip, 38.1 mi. (61.5 km)
Elevation gain: 2,260 ft.
Elevation loss: 2,260 ft.
Maximum elevation: 5,780 ft.
Difficulty: Moderate*
Topo maps: Nyack, Stanton Lake, Mt. Jackson, Mt. Stimson, Mt. St. Nicholas
Finding the trailhead: Nyack Creek ford or Coal Creek ford, both of which are accessible from U.S. Highway 2 east of West Glacier. Please ask for a detailed map of fords at Apgar Visitor Center.

*Trail is often difficult to follow, and river and stream crossings are hazardous during high water period.

0.0 Nyack Creek ford. Blazed trail starts from north bank of Middle Fork of the Flathead River.
0.1 Trail Sign. Turn left for Nyack Creek. Trail follows the Middle Fork, crossing Nyack Creek just before junction.
0.8 Junction with Nyack trail. Turn right for Nyack Creek. Trail climbs gently, following the west bank of Nyack Creek.
5.4 Lower Nyack campground.
7.4 Lower Nyack patrol cabin.
14.4 Upper Nyack campground.
15.5 Upper Nyack patrol cabin.
17.0 Junction with Cutbank Pass trail. Stay right for Coal Creek.
19.2 Trail leaves Nyack valley and begins moderate ascent to Surprise Pass.
21.7 Surprise Pass.

Mt. Stimson from Upper Nyack Creek.

22.4 Junction with Martha's Basin trail. Turn right for Buffalo Woman Lake (1.6 mi.) or Beaver Woman Lake campground (2.1 mi.) Keep left for Coal Creek. Trail descends Coal Creek valley, fording the creek five times.

31.2 Coal Creek campground. Junction with Fielding-Coal Creek trail. Stay right for Coal Creek ford. Trail continues gradual descent, fording Coal Creek once.

33.3 Coal Creek patrol cabin.

36.9 Junction with Boundary trail. Stay left for Coal Creek ford (0.4 mi.). Turn right for Nyack Creek ford.

38.0 Junction with Nyack Creek ford connector trail. Turn right for the ford.

38.1 Nyack Creek ford of the Middle Fork.

The trail: The Nyack-Coal Creek Loop provides the primary access route into and through the Nyack wilderness camping zone, with a spur trail to Cut Bank Pass linking it to trails in the Two Medicine area. Minimum-impact camping is permitted anywhere within the wilderness zone with a few basic restrictions. Developed campsites are also available in the wilderness zone through the normal permit process. Fishing in the area's streams is not permitted. Trails tend to be brushy and hard to find, and the traveler should expect to encounter obstacles such as knee-deep fords and blowdowns on this trail. The Nyack wilderness offers the most primitive hiking conditions found anywhere in the park and is not recommended for inexperienced hikers.

The loop begins at the Nyack ford of the Middle Fork of the Flathead (detailed maps of river fords are available at the Apgar Visitor Center), and joins the South Boundary trail at the old Nyack Ranger Station site. After following the river valley northwest for .5 mile, the trail crosses Nyack Creek via a suspension bridge and reaches the junction with the Nyack Creek trail. Loop hikers turn eastward here, ascending gentle benches clad with mature forest and a brushy understory above the north bank of the creek. The trail passes through many quagmires before reaching the rim of a steep, forested canyon through which the rushing torrent of Nyack Creek makes its way. After 4.5 miles, the trail reaches the Lower Nyack campground, set among towering old-growth larches and cottonwoods.

For the next seven miles the trail winds up the wooded valley, with occasional clearings that allow the hiker to view the rocky faces of Threesuns Mountain and Mt. Stimson. About 1.5 miles beyond the lower patrol cabin, the trail fords a large seasonal tributary and then hugs the sidehill while continuing up the west bank of Nyack Creek. At mile 12.8 of the loop, the trail fords Nyack Creek twice and then doglegs to the east. High winds in the winter of 1988-1989 have blown down most of the trees in this area, opening up sweeping views of Blackfoot Mountain and the Pumpelly Glacier to the northwest, as well as Mt. Stimson to the south and the peaks around Cut Bank Pass to the east. The trail climbs gently through thick brush for another 1.5 miles to the Upper Nyack campground, with its wooded setting on the fringe of a large gravel wash that provides spectacular views in all directions.

As the trail approaches the Upper Nyack cabin, it passes along the rim of yet another steep canyon. The trail winds through pleasant forest for several miles before reaching the Cut Bank Pass trail junction, at which it opens up into the brushy swampland of the upper creek bottoms. After several miles of mucky going through the brush, the trail fords Nyack Creek and enters an old-growth spruce stand. The trail reaches a sizeable tributary coming in from the south and turns up the west bank for several hundred yards before crossing it and following up the north bank. A trail was planned to cover the distance from this point up the main valley to Nyack Lake but was never completed and is not worth looking for. After switching back several times up a mild hill past cascading waterfalls, the trail levels out and begins a long, gradual ascent to Surprise Pass.

As the trail emerges into open avalanche fields, it crosses and recrosses the small creek, finally disappearing into a stand of subalpine fir slightly to the west of the valley's floor. From here, the trail passes through open forest with a copious understory of huckleberries, which make delicious eating when in season. The trail crosses the marked summit of Surprise Pass and descends almost imperceptibly to the Martha's Basin trail junction at the head of the Coal Creek Valley.

Martha's Basin Option. The Martha's Basin trail crosses the headwaters of Coal Creek to climb gradually through fields of beargrass into a cirque that lies between Mt. Pinchot and Peril Peak. After about a mile, the trail forks. The left fork climbs .5 mile to Buffalo Woman Lake, which lies below rugged Peril Peak. The right fork descends gently across an old burn for .7 mile to a campground at Beaver Woman Lake. The campground, set among old spruce trees, shows the wear and tear of years of use by horse parties.

After reaching the Martha's Basin junction, the loop trail (hereafter officially designated the Coal Creek trail) descends the steep, brushy Coal Creek valley to the southeast. Shortly before the valley doglegs to the southwest, the trail crosses Coal Creek at the first of five major fords that exist between Surprise Pass and the Coal Creek campground. From this ford, it's about five miles of hiking through mostly unspectacular bottomland to Elk Creek, on which the campground is located. The trail crosses several talus slopes shortly before reaching the campground, and these openings afford views of precipitous Mt. St. Nicholas across the valley. At the campground, the Fielding-Coal Creek trail enters the loop from the south.

Leaving the campground, the loop trail runs along the north bank of Coal Creek for two more miles before crossing one final ford just before reaching the Coal Creek patrol cabin. From this point, the valley widens, opening into the charred snags of the 1984 fire. The trail winds on high benches above the creek for 3.6 miles before reaching a junction with the South Boundary trail. By bearing to the south, hikers can reach the Coal Creek ford of the Middle Fork after a distance of .4 mile, thereby accessing U.S. Highway 2 about sixteen miles east of West Glacier. Hikers wishing to complete the loop by trail should turn north onto the South Boundary trail to return to the Nyack ford. This section of the Boundary trail was extremely difficult to find at the time this book was written; it has been upgraded and is now much easier to follow.

The boundary trail completing the loop runs down to the mouth of Coal Creek, where it fords the creek just above the site of an old bridge.

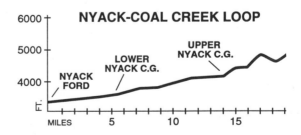

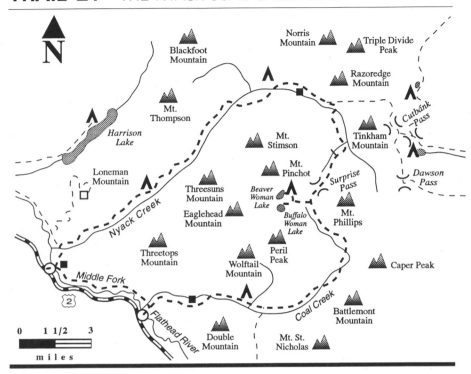

After crossing the creek, the trail hugs the Middle Fork fairly closely, dipping into a small dale to cross a tiny tributary of the river. The trail then enters unburned forest, where it is fairly obvious, rising and falling as it winds along the river, always to the south (or river) side of the small hillocks on the river's north shore. About half a mile from the Nyack Ranger Station, the trail skirts the south edge of a large meadow, where the only signs of a trail are orange disks nailed to trees at odd intervals. From this point, it is easy to bushwhack to the ranger station, if one gets lost, by skirting the meadow's south edge and bearing due west.

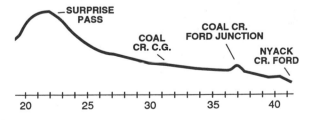

TRAIL 22 *LAKE ISABEL*

General description: A backpack from Walton R. S. to Lake Isabel, 16.9 mi. (27 km)
Elevation gain: 1,915 ft.
Maximum elevation: 5,835 ft.
Difficulty: Moderate
Topo maps: Essex, Blacktail, Mt. Rockwell
Finding the trailhead: Trail departs from the north end of the Walton Ranger Station complex, which is located on U.S. Highway 2 at the southernmost extremity of the park.

0.0 Trail sign. Trail climbs moderately, as it runs northwest following the Middle Fork of the Flathead River.
1.1 Junction with Ole Creek trail. Stay left for Lake Isabel.
1.5 Junction with Scalplock Lookout trail. Stay left for Lake Isabel.
3.2 Trail leaves the Middle Fork, turning northeast up the Park Creek valley.
7.2 Lower Park Creek campground. Junction with Fielding-Coal Creek trail. The trail to Lake Isabel and Two Medicine Pass exits campground to the north of patrol cabin. Trail ascends gently, following Park Creek. Ford of creek immediately before campground.
14.6 Upper Park Creek campground. Junction with Two Medicine Pass trail (3.8 mi. to pass). Stay left for Lake Isabel. Trail climbs moderately to the north.
16.9 Lake Isabel campground.

The trail: Lake Isabel is a subalpine cirque lake that sits at the base of Vigil Peak. Because the trail to the lake is long and somewhat tedious, the lake receives few visitors and thus is a prime destination for hikers seeking solitude. A trail connects the Park Creek trail with the Two Medicine country via Two

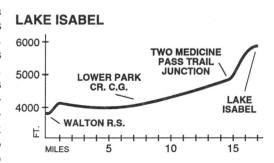

Medicine Pass, providing interesting options for backpackers with extended itineraries. Lake Isabel can also be accessed by a shorter route from Two Medicine via Cobalt Lake.

The trail begins at the Walton Ranger Station and follows the South Boundary route for 3.2 miles as it climbs the hillsides above the Middle Fork of the Flathead. The snowy Flathead Range can be seen to the south through openings in the forest. The trail descends gently to the flat top of a high bluff overlooking the river and passes among the huge boles of old-growth larches and Douglas-firs before turning east up the Park Creek valley.

After passing along forested hillsides for several miles, the trail emerges into swampy meadows of tall grass and cow parsnip, from which the low foothills

TRAILS 22 and 23 *LAKE ISABEL, SCALPLOCK LOOKOUT*

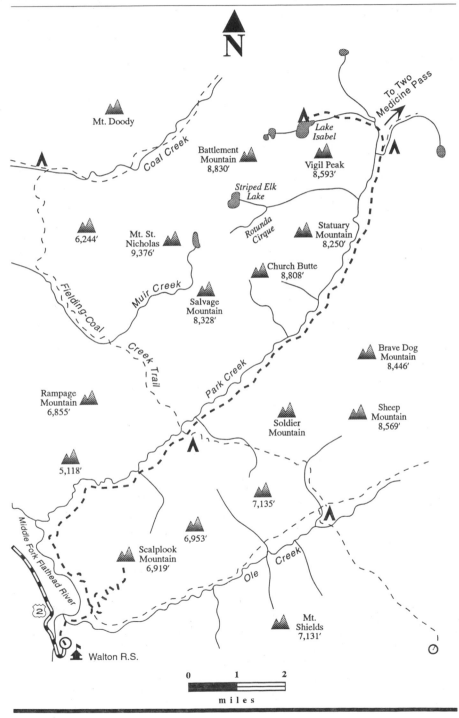

N

To Two Medicine Pass

Mt. Doody

Coal Creek

Battlement Mountain 8,830'

Lake Isabel

Vigil Peak 8,593'

Striped Elk Lake

6,244'

Mt. St. Nicholas 9,376'

Rotunda Cirque

Statuary Mountain 8,250'

Church Butte 8,808'

Muir Creek

Fielding-Coal

Salvage Mountain 8,328'

Creek Trail

Park Creek

Brave Dog Mountain 8,446'

Rampage Mountain 6,855'

5,118'

Soldier Mountain

Sheep Mountain 8,569'

7,135'

6,953'

Middle Fork Flathead River

Scalplook Mountain 6,919'

Ole Creek

2

Mt. Shields 7,131'

Walton R.S.

0   1   2

m i l e s

Lake Isabel and Battlement Mountain.

of the Lewis Range can be seen on all sides. Four miles beyond the mouth of the valley lies the Lower Park Creek campground, set in grassy meadows at the junction with the Fielding-Coal Creek trail. The trail exits the campground around the north wall of the patrol cabin and continues west through jungles of cow parsnip before climbing gently onto hills that crowd the creek as the valley becomes narrower. As one passes through closed-canopy stands of Douglas-fir, black bears may be sighted digging for roots along the trail. Avalanche chutes occasionally interrupt the canopy, allowing views of rugged Salvage Mtn. and Church Butte to the north.

Some 7.4 miles beyond the lower campground, the trail crosses a knee-deep, still-water ford before passing beside a patrol cabin into the Upper Park Creek campground. At this point, the trail forks, with the right fork climbing steeply to Two Medicine Pass and the left fork winding around to the west on its way to Lake Isabel. The trail crosses the west branch of Park Creek over a wooden bridge and ascends moderately for a distance of one mile across marshy hillsides covered with mountain ash. The trail then enters the vale of Lake Isabel's outlet stream, which it crosses and follows to the foot of the lake. At the east end of the lake, the trail passes among the twisted wrecks of trees brought down by an avalanche during the winter of 1989-1990. The campground lies on the north side of the lake, about one-third mile from its foot. There is good fishing for rainbow trout in the ten- to twelve-inch class right from the campground. Observant hikers may see evidence of grizzly bear activity around the lake.

TRAIL 23 *SCALPLOCK LOOKOUT* see p. 61 for map

General description: A day hike from Walton R.S. to Scalplock Lookout, 4.7 mi. (7.5 km)
Elevation gain: 3,079 ft.
Maximum elevation: 6,919 ft.
Difficulty: Moderate
Topo map: Essex
Finding the trailhead: Izaak Walton Ranger Station trailhead.

0.0 Trail sign. Trail ascends gradually, following the Middle Fork of the Flathead.
1.1 Junction with Ole Creek trail. Stay left for Scalplock Lookout.
1.5 Junction with Scalplock Lookout trail. Turn right for Scalplock Lookout. Trail climbs rather steeply up the flanks of Scalplock Mountain.
4.7 Scalplock Lookout.

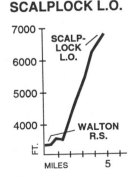

The trail: Scalplock Lookout sits high above the townsite of Essex, at the far southern tip of Glacier Park. After leaving the south Boundary trail, the Scalplock trail climbs steeply, switching back frequently across pine forest and grassy meadows to the summit. The lookout overlooks the south end of the Flathead Range to the west, with Marion Lake nestled unseen in its foothills.

To the south, the snow-capped peaks of the Bob Marshall Wilderness stretch away as far as the eye can see. Mount St. Nicholas, Salvage Mountain, and Church Butte rise to the immediate north, with other peaks of the Lewis Range behind them.

TRAIL 24 *FIREBRAND PASS-OLE LAKE*

General description: A day hike or backpack from the Lubec trailhead to Ole Lake, 7.7 mi. (11 km), or from the Lubec trailhead to Firebrand Pass, 4.8 mi. (7.5 km)
Elevation gain: 2,210 ft.
Elevation loss: 2,680 ft.
Maximum elevation: 6,951 ft.
Difficulty: Moderately strenuous
Topo maps: Summit, Squaw Mtn., Mt. Rockwell
Finding the trailhead: At mile marker 203 on US 2, follow the dirt road across the railroad tracks to a barricaded dirt road that runs for .5 mile to the site of the old Lubec Ranger Station (which was burned in 1980). The Firebrand Pass trail begins at this site.

0.0 Trail sign. Trail climbs gently, following Coonsa Creek.
1.4 Junction with Autumn Creek trail. Turn right for Firebrand Pass. Trail sidehills along the flanks of Calf Robe Mountain.
2.4 Junction with Firebrand Pass trail. Turn left for Firebrand Pass. Trail ascends rather steeply around the northeast face of Firebrand Pass.
4.8 Firebrand Pass. Trail descends steeply to Ole Lake.
7.7 Ole Lake campground.

The trail: The Firebrand Pass trail begins at a false summit near Marias Pass and winds around Calf Robe Mountain to Firebrand Pass before dropping down into the Ole Creek Valley. Ole Lake can also be reached via a longer, less scenic route up the Ole Creek valley from the Walton Ranger Station or from the Fielding trailhead. Firebrand Pass makes a reasonable destination for day hikers, while backpackers will find backcountry campsites at Ole Lake.

**FIREBRAND PASS-
OLE LAKE**

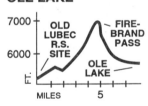

The trail starts out on the north bank of Coonsa Creek, which it follows for half a mile before turning slightly north and climbing gently to the junction with the Autumn Creek trail. Hikers bound for the pass should turn north at this junction and follow the Autumn Creek trail for one mile as it leaves the forest and enters grassy meadows near the junction with the Firebrand Pass trail, which takes off to the west. Following the Firebrand Pass trail as it winds upward around the open slopes of Calf Robe Mountain, hikers will see Squaw Mountain straight ahead and Red Crow Mountain as the trail reaches the north slope of Calf Robe. The forest on both sides of the pass burned in the hot fires of the early 1900s.

Rounding the north ridge of Calf Robe Mountain, the trail passes above the headwaters of Railroad Creek, represented by an unnamed tarn occupying the

TRAIL 24 *FIREBRAND PASS-OLE LAKE*

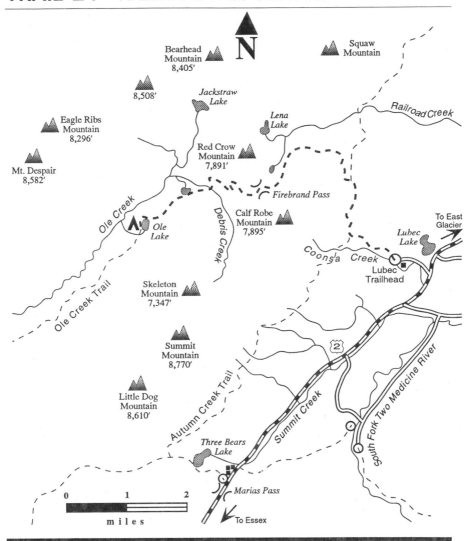

floor of a small basin below the pass. The trail climbs fairly steeply, angling to the southwest to the pass. Views from the pass include the rugged country surrounding the headwaters of Ole Creek, as well as the mountains immediately surrounding the pass. From the pass, the trail descends steeply down an open slope to Debris Creek, which it crosses, and runs westward along a wooded bench above Ole Creek. After half a mile, the trail passes an unnamed pond and continues along the bench for one mile to Ole Lake. The trail passes around the north shore of the lake to a campground, and then crosses the outlet stream and begins the long, slow descent to the floor of the Ole Creek Valley. From Ole Lake, the Ole Creek trail begins its long, tedious descent of 15.5 miles to the Izaak Walton Ranger Station.

The **South Boundary trail** from West Glacier along the Middle Fork of the Flathead to Izaak Walton Ranger Station varies in condition in different localities. It is in good condition between West Glacier and the old Nyack Ranger Station but is poorly maintained (bring a compass) between Nyack and Coal creeks, as it disappears in the large meadow southeast of the old Nyack Ranger Station. At this point, bear toward the river, to the west of the meadow and pass the low hill on the river side. As the trail enters the woods it becomes more distinct; keep your eyes peeled for round orange blaze markers on tree trunks to find the trail. Between Coal Creek and Park Creek, the trail has been washed out and abandoned entirely, so it is useless to try to follow it. Between Park Creek and Izaak Walton, the trail is well maintained and easily followed.

The trails to **Pinchot Creek** have been abandoned and can no longer be found.

The **Fielding-Coal Creek trail** connects the drainages of Bear, Ole, Park, Muir, and Coal creeks several miles above their confluences with the Middle Fork. This trail is well maintained from its beginning at the end of a primitive dirt road, #1066 near the Bear Creek Guest House, to the lower Park Creek campground and is poorly maintained from this point to the Coal Creek campground. The trail climbs gently over a low saddle, three miles long, between Bear and Ole creeks, jogs east with the Ole Creek trail for .2 mile, and then resumes its course over a more strenuous saddle below Soldier Mountain 4.5 miles to Park Creek. From this point, the trail crosses Park Creek and climbs steeply to a saddle behind Rampage Mountain, follows Muir Creek for three miles, and then climbs over a slightly lower saddle for 1.8 miles before dropping the final 1.5 miles to Coal Creek.

The **Cut Bank access trail** begins at Pitamakan Pass and crosses over Cutbank Pass before descending steeply 5.4 miles to join the Nyack Creek trail 2.6 miles above the Upper Nyack campground. The trail is poorly maintained and hard to follow in some places, so is not recommended for inexperienced hikers or horse parties.

The **Ole Creek trail** is a well-maintained, if somewhat less than scenic, trail that runs for 15.5 miles up a forested valley to Ole Lake, and then continues to Firebrand Pass.

The **Autumn Creek trail** offers day hike possibilities in the Marias Pass area. The trail begins on the west bank of Autumn Creek as it enters Bear Creek west of the Blacktail Hills, on U.S. Hwy. 2. The trail is well maintained as it climbs moderately for 1.6 miles to a low, open saddle below Elk Mountain and then descends 2.4 miles to the junction with a connector trail that runs for a mile past Three Bears Lake to the highway summit of Marias Pass. The trail is poorly maintained for the next 6.2 miles to the junction with the Lubec connector trail, which returns to Highway 2 at the old Lubec Ranger Station. The trail is well maintained for the next mile between the Lubec trail and the Firebrand Pass junction and 4.9 miles beyond to the park boundary. It then returns to low-maintenance status for the final 1.8 miles between the park boundary and the trail's terminus at the Midvale Creek bridge behind Glacier Park Lodge. This area is very popular with cross-country skiers in wintertime.

TWO MEDICINE

The mountains of the Two Medicine area were known as "the Backbone of the World" to the Blackfeet Indians, who used the area for vision quests as well as hunting and gathering. The towering spires and sheer cliff walls still provide an awe-inspiring atmosphere for travelers in search of a haven from the hurried pace of the modern world. A well-worn network of trails provides access to peaceful lakes and dizzying heights, through a landscape of unequaled beauty.

In this part of the park, sheer mountains rise abruptly from the rolling prairies of the Great Plains, providing a mixture of flora and fauna from widely different biotic communities. Alpine communities of the higher elevations grade into grasslands adapted to the more arid plains. The mountains of the divide form a barrier to moisture-laden maritime air masses, and thus this area is said to be in a *rain shadow*. Precipitation on the plains falls mostly in the summer in the form of brief thunderstorms, following the rainfall regime of the high plains. This pattern of precipitation favors shallow-rooted grasses over larger trees and shrubs, thus accounting for the lack of lush forests on this side of the Divide.

Dry winds roar through the high mountain passes and are a dominant force in shaping the patterns of vegetation in the Front Ranges. These same winds reach speeds upwards of eighty miles per hour and cause incredibly high wind-chill factors in the winter.

Wildlife in this area reflects the drier nature of the vegetation. Bighorn sheep, favoring grasses as forage, are seen more commonly in this drier area than are mountain goats. Golden eagles are not uncommon, soaring on updrafts created by the warmth of the sun on open grasslands. Waterfalls

Mt. Sinopah above Two Medicine Lake.

block the immigration of native fish into most of the lakes—fish found in most lakes were introduced at some time during the past. These planted fish have successfully occupied a vacant niche in the lake ecosystems and now sustain their populations naturally, without the aid of supplementary plantings by the National Park Service.

TRAIL 25 *SCENIC POINT*

General description: A half-day hike from Two Medicine Road to Scenic Point, 3.1 mi. (5 km), or from Two Medicine Road to East Glacier, 10.0 mi. (16 km.)
Elevation gain: 2,242 ft.
Maximum elevation: 7,522 ft.
Difficulty: Moderately strenuous
Topo map: Squaw Mtn.
Finding the trailhead: Trail departs from a marked trailhead on the Two Medicine road, approximately 11.5 miles west from its junction with Montana Highway 49.

0.0 Mt. Henry trailhead sign, near water tank.
0.5 Junction with Appistoki Falls trail (200 yards). Stay left for Scenic Point. Trail ascends the Appistoki valley, then climbs to Scenic Point.
3.1 Scenic point.
10.0 Trail reaches gravel road behind the golf course in East Glacier.

The trail: This trail is most commonly taken as a short hike from the Two Medicine Road to Scenic Point and back. The trail begins just off the Two Medicine road just before an old water tank on the east bank of Appistoki Creek and climbs along the creek past Appistoki Falls, and then ascends high on the arid valley wall above the creek. Looking up the desolate creek valley from this hillside, Mt. Henry rises its forbidding head to the south. The trail climbs to the summit of the wind-blown dome known as Scenic Point. On a clear

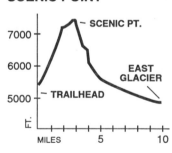

SCENIC POINT

day, the hiker can see out across the high plains all the way to the Sweetgrass Hills, some 100 miles distant. Looking to the west, Dawson Pass is clearly visible, with jagged peaks surrounding it. Only the most hardy plants grow in the arid, windswept environment on top of Scenic Point, and the poor growing conditions cause a stunted growth form in these plants.

For hikers continuing to East Glacier, the trail drops into a bowl filled with twisted trees before descending onto open slopes and crossing Fortymile Creek. The trail continues across the open east slope of the Front Range, finally descending into the trees and crossing another creek before leaving the park. The trail continues eastward, having a lower maintenance status, as it crosses a low hillock on its way to a primitive dirt road. After reaching the road,

TRAIL 25 *SCENIC POINT*

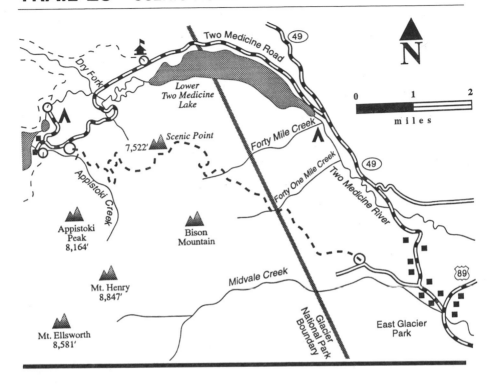

the hiker should keep a sharp eye out for trail markers, as the trail crosses several jeep roads in this area. The trail emerges from the woods onto a gravel road which reaches its terminus just north of the Glacier Park Lodge in East Glacier.

TRAIL 26 *COBALT LAKE-TWO MEDICINE PASS*

General description: A day hike or backpack from Two Medicine lower boat dock to Cobalt L., 5.7 mi. (9 km); from Two Medicine lower boat dock to junction with Park Creek trail, 12.7 mi. (20 km); or from Two Medicine upper boat dock to Cobalt Lake, 4.4 mi. (7 km)
Elevation gain: 1,400 ft.
Maximum elevation: 6,620 ft.
Difficulty: Moderate
Topo maps: Squaw Mtn., Mt. Rockwell
Finding the trailhead: South shore trailhead is located at the west end of the Two Medicine boat dock parking lot. Boat users may enter trail system at upper boat dock.

0.0 Trail sign.

0.2 Junction with Paradise Point Trail (.4 mi.). Stay left for Cobalt Lake.

1.2 Junction with Aster Falls trail (.7 mi.). Stay right for Cobalt Lake. Trail follows lakeshore loosely, crossing Paradise Creek suspension bridge.

2.3 Junction with Two Medicine Pass trail. Turn left for Cobalt Lake. Boat users enter trail here.

3.4 Rockwell Falls spur junction. Trail ascends steeply, then assumes a gradual grade to Cobalt Lake.

5.7 Cobalt Lake. Trail passes west from lakeshore, ascending to pass.

7.9 Two Medicine Pass.

12.7 Junction with Park Creek trail.

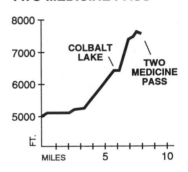

COBALT LAKE-TWO MEDICINE PASS

The trial: The Cobalt Lake trail winds around the south shore of Two Medicine Lake, ascends the valley between Sinopah Mountain and Painted Teepee Peak to Cobalt Lake, and then continues its ascent to Two Medicine Pass and drops into the Park Creek valley beyond. Rockwell Falls and Cobalt Lake are popular day hike destinations, and backcountry campsites at Cobalt Lake make more extended sojourns possible. This trail is also popular with fishermen bound for Lake Isabel in the Park Creek drainage.

The trail quits the lakeshore shortly after leaving the trailhead and ascends gently some 100 ft. through open forest. At mile .2, a spur trail takes off to the north some .4 mile to Paradise Point, a rounded promontory which offers a panoramic vista of Two Medicine Lake and the surrounding peaks. The main trail climbs through stands of subalpine fir interrupted by an occasional beaver pond for another mile to Aster Creek. After crossing Aster Creek, the south shore trail reaches the junction with the Aster Falls trail, which climbs fairly steeply .7 mile past a falls to an overlook in a narrow argillite canyon, with pleasant grassy meadows in the valley above it.

The trail continues west, crossing Paradise Creek via a suspension bridge and winding around the base of Sinopah Mountain, through brushy fields of cow parsnip and false huckleberry. At mile 3.4, the trail reaches the base of Rockwell Falls, a series of twenty-foot cascades that extends for almost half a mile up the stream's valley. After crossing the creek, the trail ascends rocky, huckleberry-clad benches beside the falls before emerging into a parkland of dwarfed firs and rock gardens. The trail ascends gently for one mile before climbing several fir-clad swales to reach a junction that leads to deep blue Cobalt Lake, at the base of Two Medicine Pass. The campground is located across the outlet of the lake, while the trail to the pass continues to the right around the north shore of the lake.

Two Medicine Pass Option. The trail ascends fairly steeply from Cobalt Lake, across open slopes beneath Mt. Rockwell, to the rounded saddle above. The trail then follows the ridgeline southward, crossing the small summit of Chief Lodgepole Peak and offering a view into Paradise Park below to the east. To the west lies the Park Creek valley, with Eagle Ribs, Mount Despair, and Brave Dog Mountain trailing away to the south. To the west lies Vigil Peak,

TRAIL 26 *COBALT LAKE-TWO MEDICINE PASS*

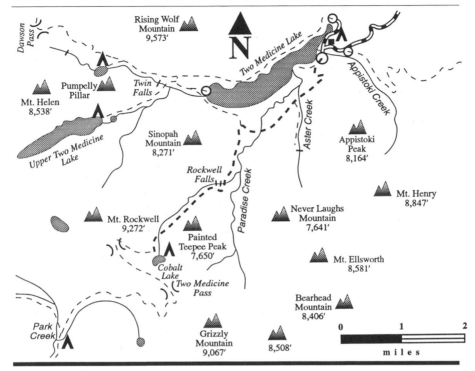

with Lake Isabel below it and the Cloudcroft Peaks in the background. From the pass, the trail descends steeply for 3.8 miles to an intersection with the Isabel Lake trail at the Upper Park Creek patrol cabin.

TRAIL 27 *UPPER TWO MEDICINE LAKE*

General description: A day hike or short backpack from the Upper boat dock to Upper Two Medicine Lake, 2.2 mi. (3.7 km), or from North Shore trailhead to Upper Two Medicine Lake, 5.0 mi. (8.0 km)
Elevation gain: 300 ft.
Maximum elevation: 5,464 ft.
Difficulty: Easy
Topo maps: Squaw Mtn., Mt. Rockwell
Finding the trailhead: Two Medicine North Shore trailhead, on the northern edge of Two Medicine campground. The trail leaves the campground over a bridge at the outlet of Pray Lake, a small pond just below Two Medicine Lake.

TRAIL 27 *UPPER TWO MEDICINE LAKE*

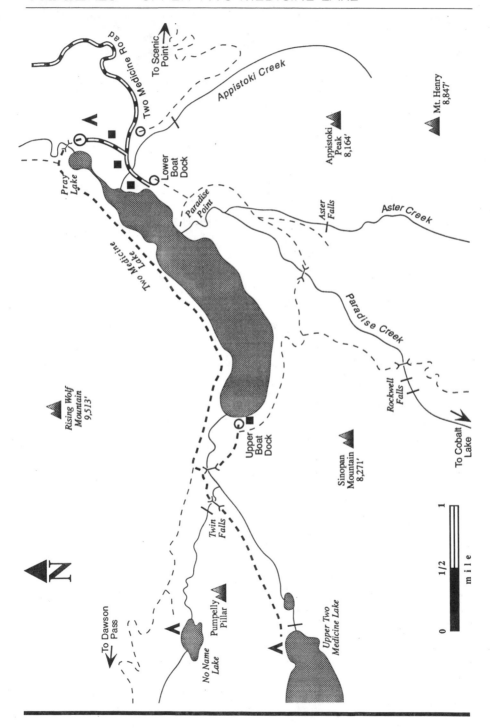

To Scenic Point

Two Medicine Road

Appistoki Creek

Mt. Henry
8,847'

Appistoki
Peak
8,164'

Pray
Lake

Lower
Boat
Dock

Paradise Point

Aster
Falls

Aster Creek

Two Medicine Lake

Paradise Creek

Rising Wolf
Mountain
9,513'

Rockwell
Falls

To Cobalt
Lake

Upper
Boat
Dock

Sinopan
Mountain
8,271'

N

Twin
Falls

To Dawson
Pass

Pumpelly
Pillar

No Name
Lake

Upper Two
Medicine Lake

0   1/2   1
mile

0.0	Trail sign. Trail follows the north shore of Two Medicine Lake.
3.3	Junction with Dawson Pass trail. Turn left for Upper Two Medicine.
3.5	Spur trail to upper boat dock. Boat users enter the trail here. Trail runs southwest, ascending almost imperceptibly.
4.6	Upper Two Medicine Lake and campground.

The trail: The Upper Two Medicine Lake trail can be reached by trail from the north or south shore trails that ring Two Medicine Lake, or by launch to the upper boat dock. The lake is a popular destination for tourists taking motor launch tours.

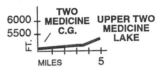

UPPER TWO MEDICINE LAKE

The launch and south shore trails run in tandem from the head of the lake up the south bank of Two Medicine Creek. Half a mile beyond the lake's head, the trail forks. The right fork connects to the north shore—Dawson Pass trail, while the left fork turns northwest to Twin Falls and Upper Two Medicine Lake. Twin Falls is a paired cascade separated by an island in mid-stream and is well worth the short side trip. The main trail continues westward, through sparse forests to the foot of the lake, where it reaches a backcountry campground. The lake is nestled among sheer peaks of red argillite, from north to south: Pumpelly Pillar, Mt. Helen, Lone Walker Mountain, and Rising Bull Ridge. This lake is good fishing for brook and rainbow trout, and mountain goats are often seen capering about on rocky ledges around the lake.

TRAIL 28 *DAWSON-PITAMAKAN*

General description: A day hike or backpack from Two Medicine campground to Dawson Pass, 5.7 mi. (9 km); from upper boat dock to Dawson Pass, 3.2 mi. (5 km); round trip from Two Medicine campground, 18.8 mi. (30 km); or round trip from upper boat dock, 16.3 mi. (26 km)
Elevation gain: 2,935 ft.
Elevation loss: 2,935 ft.
Maximum elevation: 8,099 ft.
Difficulty: Moderately strenuous
Topo maps: Squaw Mtn., Mt. Rockwell, Cut Bank Pass
Finding the trailhead: Two Medicine north shore trailhead, on the north side of Two Medicine campground, at the outlet of Pray Lake. Boat travelers will begin from the upper boat dock, meeting the trail after Twin Falls.

0.0	Trail sign. Trail follows north shore of Two Medicine Lake.
3.3	Junction with trail leading to Twin Falls and the south shore trail. Stay right for Dawson Pass.
4.8	Junction with trail to No Name Lake and campground (.2 mi.). Stay right for Dawson Pass. Trail ascends steeply to Dawson Pass.
6.7	Dawson Pass. Trail runs north, following the west face of the Continental Divide.
9.9	Cutbank Pass. Junction with trail into Nyack Creek. Stay right for Pitamakan Pass.

Looking into the Upper Nyack Valley.

10.0 Pitamakan Pass. Junction with the trail down Cutbank Creek. Stay right for Oldman Lake and Two Medicine campground. Trail descends steeply toward Oldman Lake.
12.0 Oldman Lake.
12.9 Oldman campground. Trail descends gently, following the Dry Fork Creek.
16.4 Junction with Dry Fork trail. Stay right for Two Medicine campground. Trail turns south, traversing the flanks of Rising Wolf Mountain.
18.8 Two Medicine campground.

The trail: The Dawson-Pitamakan trail runs from Two Medicine Lake to the Continental Divide and around into the Dry Fork drainage to form a long loop. It offers spectacular views of the spires of the southern Lewis Range, as well as good wildlife viewing opportunities along its entire length. The trail may be hiked in its entirety in a single day, but it takes several days to fully explore the wonders of this region.

The trail begins at the Two Medicine auto campground and winds around the north shore of the lake, beneath the hulking mass of Rising Wolf Mountain. Openings provided by avalanches from the mountain above allow excellent views of the peaks across the lake. The trail winds through a mixed

TRAIL 28 *DAWSON-PITAMAKAN*

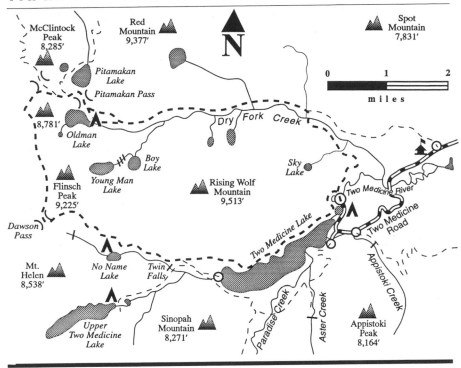

forest which grades into spruce stands before finally emerging to an opening below Sinopah Mountain at the head of the lake. At this point, a connecting trail from the south shore trail and the upper boat dock joins the Dawson Pass trail. Travelers using the tour boat enter the trail here, having cut off the first two miles of the trail. A

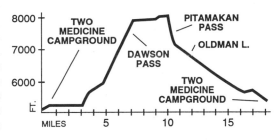

DAWSON-PITAMAKAN

short side trip of .3 mile down this connecting trail brings the hiker using the North Shore trail to Twin Falls.

From this point, the trail ascends gently into the Bighorn Basin, a glacier-carved bowl filled with scattered stands of subalpine fir and lush meadows. At mile 4.8, a spur trail descends to No Name Lake, with its attendant campground. The Dawson Pass trail continues to climb the south slope of Flinsch Peak, offering views of Mt. Helen and the knife-edge wall of the Pumpelly Pillar. After two miles and 1,200 feet of steady climbing, the trail reaches the windy saddle of Dawson Pass. From this spot, vistas open to the glacier-carved valley of Nyack Creek to the south and the Lupfer Glacier,

TRAIL 28 *DAWSON-PITAMAKAN (PITAMAKAN PASS)*

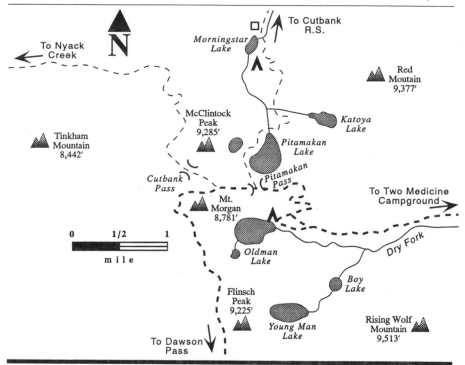

To Cutbank R.S.

To Nyack Creek

N

Morningstar Lake

Red Moutain 9,377'

McClintock Peak 9,285'

Katoya Lake

Tinkham Mountain 8,442'

Pitamakan Lake

Cutbank Pass

Pitamakan Pass

To Two Medicine Campground

Mt. Morgan 8,781'

0   1/2   1

m i l e

Oldman Lake

Dry Fork

Boy Lake

Flinsch Peak 9,225'

Young Man Lake

Rising Wolf Mountain 9,513'

To Dawson Pass

nestled high on the east slope of Mt. Phillips across the valley. From Dawson Pass, mountaineers will find a fairly easy ascent up the south face of Flinsch Peak to its summit.

From Dawson Pass, the trail turns north, following the Continental Divide along its west face around Flinsch Peak to an unnamed saddle at the head of the Dry Fork valley. The trail crosses dry, barren rockscapes all along the divide and backward glances reveal outstanding views of Lone Walker Mountain, Caper Peak, Battlement Mountain, and the spiny summit of Mt. St. Nicholas. This area is also home to bighorn sheep. The trail continues around Mt. Morgan, and rocky pedestals on a spur ridge provide an ideal lunch spot among breathtaking views of Mts. Stimson and Pinchot across the valley, as well as the peaks to the south and north. The trail winds around to Pitamakan overlook, which affords stunning views to the north and west.

From this point, the trail turns east, following the north slope of Mt. Morgan. A connecting trail from the Nyack wilderness rises to meet the Dawson-Pitamakan trail in the course of its gentle descent to Pitamakan (Pit-ah'-muh-kun) Pass, high above the large lake of the same name to the north. The trail to the north descends to Pitamakan Lake in the Cutbank Creek valley. Looking southward, the partial horn of Flinsch Peak soars above Oldman Lake, while pyramid-shaped Rising Wolf Mountain rises further to the east. The trail descends steeply, switching back frequently through rocky ledges covered with wildflowers and firs, reaching a spur trail to the campground at the foot of

Oldman Lake. This lake receives a fair amount of angling pressure, but remains good fishing for Yellowstone cutthroat trout in the one- to three-pound class. The campground is set in an open stand of old-growth whitebark pines, about a hundred yards east of the lakeshore.

After leaving the campground, the trail descends through parklike stands of fir separated by beargrass-studded fields along the Dry Fork. As the trail continues down the valley, it enters drier meadows of tall grasses reminiscent of high plains habitats. Nearing the foot of the valley, the trail enters a sun-dappled forest of lodgepole pine. Some 2.4 miles before reaching the Two Medicine campground, a trail forks to the east, leading 2.6 miles through marshy aspen stands to the entrance station on the Two Medicine road. The main trail swings southward, around the forested base of Rising Wolf, to terminate at the footbridge below Pray Lake.

TRAIL 29 CUTBANK CREEK

General description: A backpack from Cutbank R.S. to Morningstar Lake, 6.6 mi. (10.5 km), or from Cutbank R.S. to Pitamakan Pass, 9.8 mi. (15.5 km)
Elevation gain to Morningstar Lake: 640 ft.
Elevation gain to Pitamakan Pass: 2,515 ft.
Maximum elevation: 7,557 ft. (Pitamakan Pass)
Difficulty: Easy (to Morningstar); moderately strenuous (to Pitamakan Pass)
Topo map: Cutbank Pass
Finding the trailhead: Take Montana Highway 49 to junction with Cutbank Creek Road, seventeen miles north of East Glacier. Drive four miles over this improved gravel road past ranger station to the backcountry parking area. Trail runs west from this parking lot.

0.0	Trail sign. Trail ascends gently, following the North Fork of Cutbank Creek.
0.1	Junction with old Cutbank Chalet access road. Stay right for Morningstar Lake.
3.9	Junction with Triple Divide trail (3.3 miles to Triple Divide Pass, 2.1 miles to Medicine Grizzly Lake). Stay left for Morningstar Lake. Trail turns toward the south and continues ascent of Cutbank valley.
4.1	Trail passes Atlantic Falls.
6.6	Morningstar Lake campground. Trail ascends fairly steeply, then levels off and ascends again before reaching Pitamakan Lake.
8.6	Pitamakan Lake. Trail crosses lake outlet and winds around west side of Pitamakan Lake before ascending steeply to the pass.
9.8	Pitamakan Pass.

The trail: The Cutbank Creek valley is a seldom-visited, but beautiful valley, characterized by fir parklands, rushing streams, and towering red mountains from which graceful cascades descend. The valley itself may be the ultimate goal of backpacking trips, and hikers interested in extended trips can connect to the Dawson-Pitamakan and Nyack Creek trails from junctions at Pitamakan

Oldman Lake and Flinsch Peak.

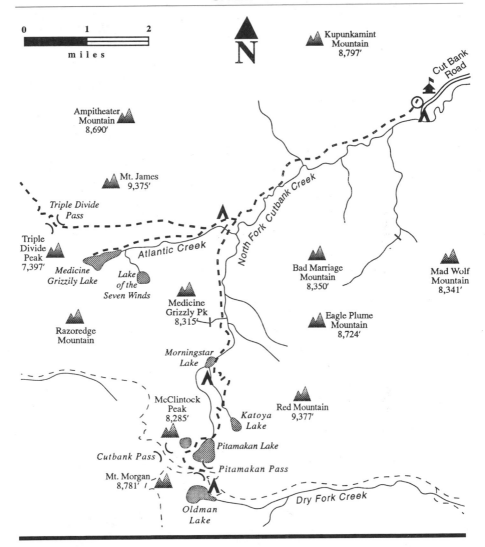

0   1   2
miles

N

Kupunkamint Mountain 8,797'

Cut Bank Road

Ampitheater Mountain 8,690'

Mt. James 9,375'

Triple Divide Pass

Triple Divide Peak 7,397'

Atlantic Creek

North Fork Cutbank Creek

Medicine Grizzily Lake

Lake of the Seven Winds

Medicine Grizzly Pk 8,315'

Razoredge Mountain

Bad Marriage Mountain 8,350'

Mad Wolf Mountain 8,341'

Eagle Plume Mountain 8,724'

Morningstar Lake

McClintock Peak 8,285'

Katoya Lake

Red Mountain 9,377'

Cutbank Pass

Pitamakan Lake

Pitamakan Pass

Mt. Morgan 8,781'

Dry Fork Creek

Oldman Lake

Pass and Cut Bank Pass. Triple Divide Pass provides access to the St. Mary valley to the north.

The trail begins just beyond the Cutbank Ranger Station, on a well-maintained gravel road. The trail crosses low-elevation meadows before entering an open forest of lodgepole pine and Douglas-fir. The trail climbs imperceptibly as it follows the north bank of the creek, and openings in the trees

CUTBANK CREEK

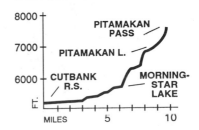

8000 — PITAMAKAN PASS

7000 — PITAMAKAN L.

6000 — CUTBANK R.S. / MORNING-STAR LAKE

FT.

MILES   5   10

Bad Marriage Mountain.

reveal a small, rocky canyon as the creek passes below the foot of Bad Marriage Mountain. The process of frost cracking is constantly at work on this mountain. During the winter, water seeps into cracks in the rock. As the water freezes, it expands, creating a wedge which separates large chunks of rock from the parent material. The huge aprons of dislodged boulders below cliff faces called *talus* slopes are a testimony to the powerful impact of this process on local landforms. Game trails can be seen crossing the talus slope at the base of this mountain, which is a good place to look for bighorn sheep.

About four miles up the trail, there is a junction with the Triple Divide Pass and Medicine Grizzly Lake trail, beyond a beaver pond populated with fingerling trout. There is a cache pole to the east of this junction, so that backpackers can hang their gear and take a day hike to one of these two destinations. From this trail junction the trail turns south, crossing Atlantic Creek immediately below Atlantic Falls, a small but charming waterfall in a pleasant woodland setting. The trail enters an open, meadowy valley filled with wildflowers, and the red argillite massifs of Eagle Plume and Red Mountain are prominent to the east. As the trail passes in the shadow of Medicine Grizzly Peak, a series of waterfalls cascade from a hidden cirque high above to the valley floor.

After a moderate ascent through subalpine fir forest, the trail winds through tiny meadows created by long-lasting snowbanks. Only small plants that grow rapidly, such as the glacier lily, can take advantage of the short, snow-free growing season found in these tiny spots. The trail then reaches the shore of Morningstar Lake, a shallow, glassy body of water that lies at the base of sheer cliff walls. After crossing the lake's outlet, the trail winds around its eastern shore to a pleasant campground at the head of the lake.

From Morningstar Lake, the trail ascends fairly steeply through stunted trees and grassy meadows to the outlet stream of Katoya Lake, a lovely lake nestled among blocky cliffs which is reached via a short bushwhack upstream from the trail. After crossing this stream, the trail ascends again for half a mile to the next shelf, which it follows to Pitamakan Lake. This section of the trail often harbors deep snowdrifts into the summer, and the lake often contains twisted icebergs left over from the winter's icepack.

The trail crosses the outlet of Pitamakan Lake and ascends a sparsely wooded spur ridge to the north wall of the cirque, where it switches back repeatedly through gravelly wastes and alpine tundra toward the pass. The trail overlooks Lake of the Seven Winds at the foot of McClintock Peak before emerging on the rounded saddle of Pitamakan Pass, with its spectacular view of rugged Flinsch Peak and Rising Wolf Mountain, with the sapphire pool of Oldman Lake below them.

TRAIL 30 MEDICINE GRIZZLY LAKE-TRIPLE DIVIDE PASS
see p. 79 for map

General description: A day hike or short backpack from Cutbank R.S. to Medicine Grizzly Lake, 6.0 mi. (9.5 km), or from Cutbank R.S. to Triple Divide Pass, 7.2 mi. (11.5 km)
Elevation gain to Medicine Grizzly Lake: 540 ft.
Elevation gain to Triple Divide Pass: 2,380 ft.
Maximum elevation: 7,397 ft. (Triple Divide Pass)
Difficulty: Easy (Medicine Grizzly); moderate (Triple Divide Pass)
Topo maps: Cut Bank Pass, Mt. Stimson
Finding the trailhead: Trail departs from a parking lot just beyond the Cutbank Ranger Station. See Cutbank Creek for details.

0.0 Trail sign. Trail climbs gently, following the North Fork of Cutbank Creek.
1.0 Junction with old chalet road. Stay right for Medicine Grizzly Lake and Triple Divide Pass.
3.9 Junction with Triple Divide trail. Turn right for the pass and Medicine Grizzly Lake. Trail begins gradual ascent of Atlantic Creek valley.
4.3 Atlantic Creek campground.
4.6 Junction with Medicine Grizzly trail. Turn left for Medicine Grizzly Lake (1.4 mi.). Stay right for Triple Divide Pass. Trail climbs north side of Atlantic Creek valley.
7.2 Triple Divide Pass.

The trail: The Triple Divide Pass trail begins at the Cutbank Creek Ranger Station and follows Cutbank Creek for almost four miles before ascending the Atlantic Creek valley. Both Medicine Grizzly Lake and Triple Divide Pass may be visited on a long day hike, while a campground near the confluence of Atlantic and Cutbank creeks provides overnight facilities for backpackers. Triple Divide Pass connects the Cutbank Creek trail with the Red Eagle Lake trail, allowing access for hikers on extended trips into the St. Mary

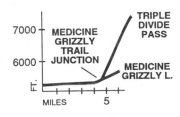

TRIPLE DIVIDE PASS

Hiker and marmot below Triple Divide Peak.

Split Mountain from Triple Divide Pass.

drainage. A trail description for the first four miles can be found in the description of the Cutbank Creek trail.

From the trail junction at Atlantic Creek, the Triple Divide trail climbs gently to the north, passing through the Atlantic Creek campground. Two-thirds of a mile from the junction, the trail forks, with the left fork following the valley floor for 1.4 miles through beargrass-studded parklands to Medicine Grizzly Lake. The right fork rises steadily along the north wall of the valley, climbing high above Medicine Grizzly Lake. Across the valley, an unnamed lake lies in a hanging cirque embedded in the north face of Medicine Grizzly Peak. The trail continues its pleasant grade upward without a single switchback, passing tiny waterfalls and emerging into a meadowy bowl below the pass.

Triple Divide Pass derives its moniker from the peak of the same name that overlooks the pass to the west. Water flowing from the various sides of this peak will eventually reach the Atlantic, Pacific, and Arctic oceans. An alpinist's route to the peak's summit crosses the steep talus bowl to the south and climbs the second of two couloirs, which pierces the Atlantic valley headwall to reach a flat saddle. From this point, it is an easy scramble up the south slope of the peak to the summit.

Wildlife is abundant in the vicinity of the pass. Hoary marmots, chipmunks, and both golden-mantled and Columbia ground squirrels make their homes in the talus surrounding the pass. Bighorn sheep are frequently sighted on the surrounding slopes. Herds of bighorn are segregated by sex—rams and ewes are rarely found in the same herd during the summer months. These animals begin rutting in September, and the thunderous cracks of colliding rams may be heard as early as late August. Looking northward from the pass, Norris Mountain dominates the head of the valley, while Split Mountain rises on its northern perimeter. The south faces of the peaks surrounding Little Chief Mountain can be seen in the background.

A short spur runs from the Two Medicine South Shore trail to **Paradise Point**, a total distance of .6 mile. The hike is an easy one, over fairly flat ground and passes through fir forest past several beaver ponds on the way to its destination on the lakeshore.

Another spur trail from the south shore trail runs up a ravine to **Aster Falls**. The total distance from the east boat dock to the end of the trail is 1.9 miles. Above the falls is an open meadow known as Aster Park, which affords a pleasant spot for a picnic.

The **Cutbank Pass trail** connects Pitamakan Pass to the Nyack Valley, allowing east-west crossings of the Continental Divide in the park's southern areas. This connector is very steep and thus is not recommended for horse parties or the faint-hearted.

A trail running south from Rockwell Falls to **Paradise Park** is still shown on some maps. This trail is not in existence, however, and it requires a real bushwhack to reach this area.

A short administrative trail runs for a mile from the Cutbank Ranger Station to **Milk River Ridge** on the park boundary. This trail has little to recommend it in terms of scenery. Another administrative trail takes off from the old chalet site and runs up the ridge to Mad Wolf Mountain.

THE ST. MARY VALLEY

The St. Mary River drainage is bisected by the Going-to-the-Sun Highway, which provides easy access for hikers and backpackers. The most dominant feature of the area is St. Mary Lake itself, which reflects a number of stunning vistas of the mountains surrounding it. The front ranges are formed of Grinnell argillite, which imparts a characteristic reddish tint to the peaks. The rain shadow formed by the Continental Divide explains the lack of snow on the eastern peaks during July and August. The peaks along the backbone of the divide are characteristically clad in snow year round, and a few small glaciers remain in the higher cirques that hark back to the time when the entire park was covered in ice.

The grassy flats around Rising Sun provide important winter range for the elk that inhabit this area, and in the autumn the bugling of bulls echoes from the valley walls. The valley is dominated by lodgepole pines at the low elevations, with a few stands of aspen in areas of water-logged soil. Higher up, spruce and subalpine fir are interspersed with beargrass and other wildflowers. Dry south-facing slopes are covered with the drought-resistant grasses that dominate the high plains to the east.

The town of St. Mary provides all visitor facilities, including a first-rate lodge that serves lake whitefish, a delicacy caught in nearby lakes, on occasion. There is a visitor center just inside the park boundary where information and backcountry permits are available. Half a mile beyond the entrance station is the St. Mary auto campground. There is a motel and camp store at Rising Sun, as well as a park-run auto campground. A privately run tour boat runs tours from Rising Sun, featuring scenic and interpretive loop cruises on the lake.

TRAIL 31 RED EAGLE LAKE

General description: A day hike or backpack from St. Mary trailhead to Red Eagle L. foot, 7.5 mi. (12 km), or from St. Mary to Triple Divide Pass, 16.2 mi. (26 km)
Elevation gain to Red Eagle Lake: 300 ft.
Elevation gain to Triple Divide Pass: 2,980 ft.
Maximum elevation: 7,397 ft. (Triple Divide Pass)
Difficulty: Easy (to Red Eagle); moderately strenuous (to Triple Divide Pass)
Topo maps: St. Mary, Rising Sun, Mt. Stimson
Finding the trailhead: Take the Going-to-the-Sun Road .25 mile east from St. Mary township to a paved road entering on the south before the Entrance Station. Take this road, bearing right, about .5 mile, to a parking lot with a trailhead sign. The trail occupies an abandoned roadbed to the southwest.

0.0   Trail sign. Trail follows abandoned dirt road, abandoning the lakeshore within one mile.
1.2   Junction with trail returning to 1913 Ranger Station. Stay right for Red Eagle Lake.

Wild Goose Island on St. Mary Lake. Photo by Candice Hanson.

3.9 Trail leaves road, turning south toward Red Eagle Lake. Trail descends to Red Eagle Creek and crosses it, and then follows its north bank.

5.1 Junction with St. Mary Lake trail. Stay left for Red Eagle Lake. Trail follows Red Eagle Creek, crossing again to the south bank, then leaves the creek and cuts through forested lowlands to Red Eagle Lake.

7.5 Red Eagle Lake (foot) and campground. Trail follows eastern shore of Red Eagle Lake.

8.4 Red Eagle Lake (head) campground. Trail follows Red Eagle Creek, crossing it once.

10.1 Trail turns south, ascending the Hudson Bay Creek valley.

14.8 Trail begins fairly steep ascent to the pass.

16.2 Triple Divide Pass.

The trail: Red Eagle Lake lies in a gentle, low-elevation valley that provides surprisingly scenic hiking to the few travelers that venture this way. More adventurous hikers may choose to follow the trail all the way to Triple Divide Pass and beyond into the Cutbank Creek country. The trail passes through good grizzly bear habitat along its entire length, so appropriate precautions should be taken.

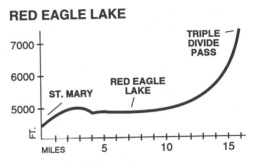

The trail starts as an old dirt road below the foot of St. Mary Lake near the old ranger station and leaves the lakeshore quickly to wind through a dense, old stand of wind-blown Douglas-firs. This road winds on through stands of

Red Eagle Lake.

TRAIL 31 *RED EAGLE LAKE*

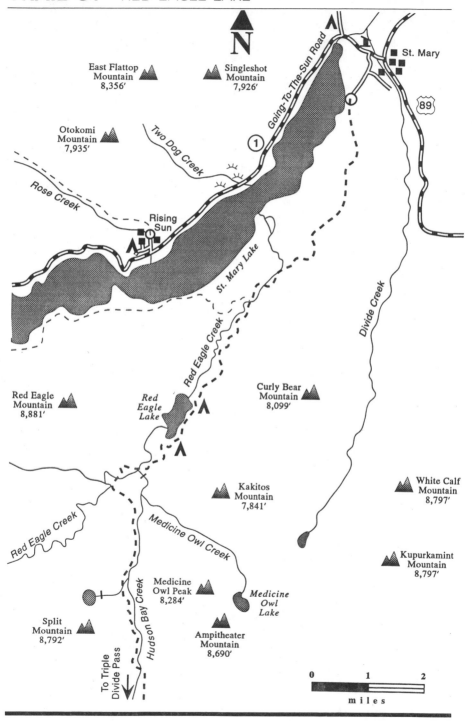

N

East Flattop
Mountain
8,356'

Singleshot
Mountain
7,926'

St. Mary

89

Otokomi
Mountain
7,935'

Two Dog Creek

Going-To-The-Sun Road

1

Rose Creek

Rising
Sun

1

St. Mary Lake

Red Eagle Creek

Divide Creek

Red Eagle
Mountain
8,881'

Red
Eagle
Lake

Curly Bear
Mountain
8,099'

Kakitos
Mountain
7,841'

White Calf
Mountain
8,797'

Red Eagle Creek

Medicine Owl Creek

Kupurkamint
Mountain
8,797'

Hudson Bay Creek

Medicine
Owl Peak
8,284'

Medicine
Owl
Lake

Split
Mountain
8,792'

Ampitheater
Mountain
8,690'

To Triple
Divide Pass

0   1   2

m i l e s

aspen and huge open meadows filled with wildflowers, which offer views of the snow-capped peaks up the St. Mary valley. At mile 3.9, the trail leaves the dirt track and descends to cross Red Eagle Creek via a suspension bridge. The trail follows the creek for 1.2 miles to a junction with the St. Mary Lake trail. The trail then re-crosses the creek and continues through open meadows and mossy forests to the foot of Red Eagle Lake, which was formed by the damming action of a sill of hard rock at the lake's outlet.

Red Eagle Lake is well known for its population of huge rainbow-cutthroat hybrid trout, as well as a few smaller brookies. Some sort of boat is needed to reach out beyond the drop-offs to where the lunkers lurk in deeper water. From the campground at the foot of the lake, one can view the craggy peaks of Norris Mountain, Split Mountain, and Logan Peak with the Red Eagle and Logan glaciers on its east face. As the trail winds around the east shore of the lake, Red Eagle Mountain's red argillite mass looms to the west. There is a second, less attractive campground at the head of the lake.

Triple Divide Pass Option. The trail continues to the south reaching Triple Divide Pass after almost eight miles. For the first mile, it follows the east bank of Red Eagle Creek, then crosses a suspension bridge upstream of several substantial waterfalls. The trail dips west, then crosses Red Eagle Creek for the final time and swings to the south to ascend the valley of Hudson Bay Creek. The trail remains fairly level, passing through old-growth forest. After three miles the forest opens into brushfields, and an impressive waterfall can be seen cascading from a cleft high on Split Mountain to the west. The reddish massifs of Medicine Owl Peak, Amphitheater Mountain, and Mount James are visible across the valley.

After crossing the unnamed creek of the aforementioned waterfall, the trail ascends through dense willows (make noise to warn off bears) and emerges into grassy parklands dotted with stands of fir. From these meadows, Norris Mountain is seen at the head of the valley, with Triple Divide Peak protruding as a knobbed ridge from its east face. This peak marks the watershed divide between the Arctic, Atlantic, and Pacific oceans. A mountaineer's route to the summit is discussed under Triple Divide Pass. The trail climbs gently to the head of the valley, where a series of babbling waterfalls cascades down a low ledge of cretaceous rock. Here the trail begins its assault of the pass in earnest, switching back across parklands and scree slopes to the pass. Talus slopes surrounding the pass are home to pikas and marmots, as well as chipmunks and several species of ground squirrel. Bands of bighorn sheep are frequently sighted on the slopes surrounding the pass. Inexperienced climbers with a taste for high places will find an easy ascent along the ridgeline to the northeast, terminating at the summit of 9,375-foot Mt. James.

TRAIL 32 *OTOKOMI LAKE*

General description: A day hike or short backpack from Rising Sun Motor Lodge to Otokomi Lake, 5.0 mi. (8 km)
Elevation gain: 1,882 ft.
Maximum elevation: 6,125 ft.
Difficulty: Moderate
Topo map: Rising Sun
Finding the trailhead: Rising Sun trailhead is located on the service road to the cabins at Rising Sun Motor Lodge. The trail leaves from the far north end of the complex. Hikers should be advised that there is no bridge over Rose Creek on the spur trail from the campground.

0.0 Trail sign.
1.5 Trail follows east bank of Rose Creek.
5.0 Otokomi Lake campground.

The trail: This trail passes up Rose Creek along the Lewis thrust fault to a low-elevation cirque lake among blocky, reddish mountains. The trail begins

TRAIL 32 *OTOKOMI LAKE*

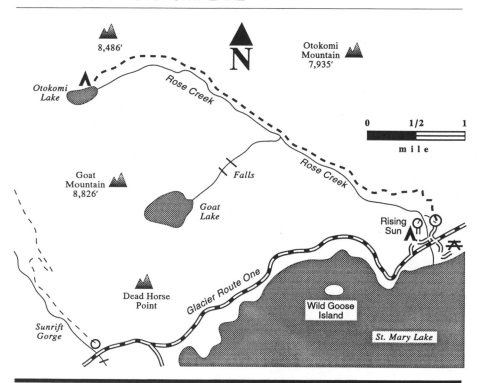

in the wooded St. Mary valley, and climbs around a hillside to the west to enter the Rose Creek drainage. After hiking along the forested creek valley for 2.5 miles past pools and small waterfalls, the hiker climbs onto an open rockslide area from which Goat Mountain is clearly visible across the lake. Just before reaching the lake, the trail passes Otokomi campground, located to the left of the trail. The trail bends around to the southwest before

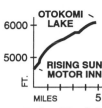

OTOKOMI L.

arriving at the outlet to Otokomi (pronounced Oh-toh¹-kum-ee) Lake. The lake covers the floor of the Rose Basin, named for the ruddy argillite cliffs surrounding the cirque.

TRAIL 33 *ST. MARY AND VIRGINIA FALLS*

General description: A half-day hike from Going-to-the-Sun Road to St. Mary Falls, 1.2 mi. (2 km), or from Going-to-the-Sun Road to Virginia Falls, 1.8 mi. (3 km)

Elevation loss: 260 ft.

Elevation gain: 285 ft.

Maximum elevation: 4,800 ft.

Difficulty: Easy

Topo map: Rising Sun

Finding the trailhead: Trailhead is located on the Going-to-the-Sun Road approximately .3 mile west of Baring Creek.

0.0   Trail sign. Trail descends toward the St. Mary River.

0.3   Junction with the Piegan Pass trail. Turn right for St. Mary Falls and Virginia Falls.

0.7   Junction with St. Mary trail. Turn left for falls.

1.2   Trail crosses St. Mary River at St. Mary Falls. Trail continues, ascending the south side of the St. Mary valley.

1.8   Virginia Falls.

The trail: This trail is a short and pleasant stroll through sun-dappled forest to several roaring waterfalls in the valley below Going-to-the-Sun Road. From the trailhead, the trail descends to the valley floor, past well-marked trail junctions to cross the river immediately below St. Mary Falls. The trail then opens up, affording views of Little Chief and Dusty Star Mountains. The path winds

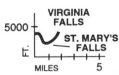

ST. MARY FALLS

around the ends of several hillocks to Virginia Creek, which it follows for half a mile past a narrow gorge to the second falls at the foot of a hanging valley.

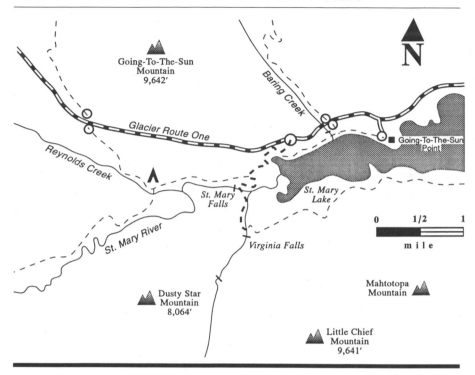

N

Going-To-The-Sun
Mountain
9,642'

Baring Creek

Glacier Route One

Reynolds Creek

Going-To-The-Sun
Point

St. Mary
Falls

St. Mary
Lake

St. Mary River

Virginia Falls

0   1/2   1

m i l e

Dusty Star
Mountain
8,064'

Mahtotopa
Mountain

Little Chief
Mountain
9,641'

St. Mary Falls.

Virginia Falls. Photo by Candice Hanson

TRAIL 34 GUNSIGHT PASS

General description: A backpack from Jackson Glacier Overlook to Lake Ellen Wilson, 10.9 mi. (17.5 km); from Overlook to Sperry Chalets, 13.6 mi. (22 km); or from Overlook to Lake McDonald, 20.0 mi. (32 km)
Elevation gain: 3,287 ft.
Elevation loss: 3,787 ft.
Maximum elevation: 7,050 ft. (Lincoln Pass)
Difficulty: Moderately strenuous (east to west), strenuous (west to east)
Topo maps: Logan Pass, Mt. Jackson, L. McDonald East
Finding the trailhead: To hike the trail from east to west, take the Going-to-the-Sun Highway east of Logan Pass to the Jackson Glacier Overlook. The Gunsight Pass trail begins at the east end of this overlook. To hike the trail from west to east, start at the Snyder Creek trailhead, which is located across the Going-to-the-Sun Road from the Lake McDonald Lodge coffee shop.

0.0 Trail sign downhill from Jackson Glacier Overlook. Trail descends toward Reynolds Creek.
1.3 Junction with Gunsight Pass trail immediately after Deadwood Falls. Turn right for Gunsight Pass. Trail begins a gentle ascent of the Reynolds Creek valley.
4.0 Junction with Florence Falls trail (.8 mi.). Stay left for Gunsight Pass. Trail ascends moderately along the flanks of Fusillade Mtn.
6.2 Gunsight Lake campground. Trail crosses Gunsight Lake outlet, then climbs steeply up the north face of Mt. Jackson.
9.2 Gunsight Pass (El. 6,946 ft.). Trail descends steeply toward Lake Ellen Wilson.
10.9 Junction with Lake Ellen Wilson campground trail (.3 mi.). Stay right for Sperry Chalets. Trail ascends steeply along the south face of Gunsight Mtn.
12.1 Lincoln Pass. Trail descends into the Glacier Basin.
13.2 Sperry campground junction.
13.3 Sperry Chalets.
13.8 Junction with Sperry Glacier Overlook trail (3.7 mi., strenuous, maximum elevation 8,000 ft.). Stay left for Lake McDonald. Trail descends steeply, following Sprague Creek, and then turns north around the end of a ridge to Snyder Creek.
18.1 Junction with Snyder Ridge trail. Stay right for Lake McDonald. Trail crosses to north bank of Snyder Creek.
18.2 Junction with Snyder Lakes trail. Stay left for Lake McDonald.
18.3 Junction with Mt. Brown Lookout trail. Stay left for Lake McDonald.
20.0 Lake McDonald Lodge.

The trail: The Gunsight Pass trail is an extremely popular backpacking route that ascends to the Continental Divide from the St. Mary valley and crosses rocky ledges and alpine meadows to Sperry Chalets before descending to Lake McDonald. The high country offers access to active glaciers, excellent fishing in subalpine lakes, and viewing opportunities for many types of wildlife. The trail can be hiked in one grueling day by a dedicated hiker, but one day is insufficient to take advantage of and appreciate the varied opportunities presented by the trail. Gunsight Pass receives heavy snow which may not melt until mid-July and thus is safest in the late summer. Because the backcountry campsites fill up quickly along this

GUNSIGHT PASS

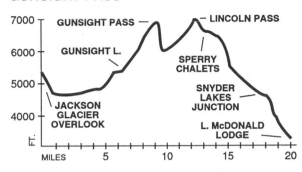

trail, backpackers should register for campsites as early as possible.

The trail begins at the Jackson Glacier overlook, and after a brief descent to the valley floor, the trail follows the meandering course of the St. Mary River. The trail winds through mossy forest and marshy openings, crossing Reynolds Creek below Deadwood Falls. To the south, the St. Mary River winds through open, grassy meadows, and Dusty Star Mountain and Citadel Mountain can be glimpsed to the south. At mile 4.0, a spur trail leads off to the west, rising gently to the base of Florence Falls, a tumbling cascade that issues from the end of the hanging valley containing Twin Lakes.

Half a mile further, the trail begins a moderate ascent up the east slope of Fusillade Mountain. Brushy avalanche slopes allow excellent views of Mounts Jackson and Logan at the head of the valley, with the extensive Jackson and Blackfoot glaciers, which were once one huge glacier, at their feet. A trail ascends toward these two glaciers, but is no longer brushed out regularly and

The "horse and rider" rising from the crest of the cliff wall, as trail nears Lincoln Pass.

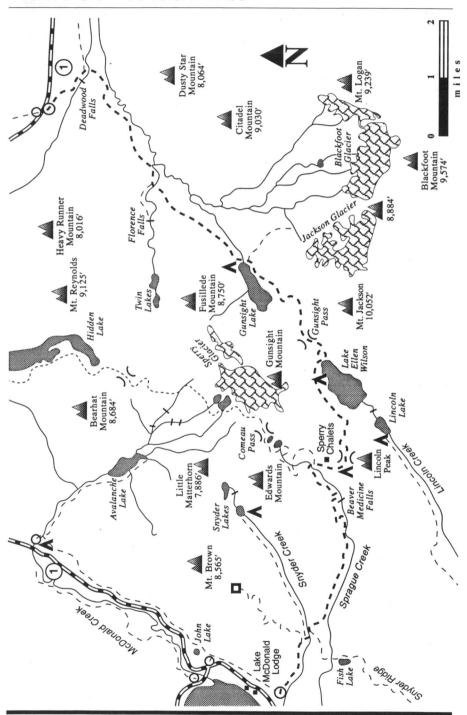

tends to disappear with disturbing frequency in jungles of cow parsnip. At mile 6.2, the trail reaches the foot of Gunsight Lake, reputed to be good fishing for rainbow trout. There is an extensive campground at the foot of this brushy lake, which is a good place to view ospreys swooping for their fishy prey.

From the foot of Gunsight Lake, the trail crosses the outlet via a suspension bridge and begins a long climb up the open north slope of Mt. Jackson to the pass almost 1,600 feet above. As the trail climbs around cliff ledges, there are outstanding views of the folded strata of Gunsight Mountain to the north. As the trail approaches the pass, it enters charming meadow vales with rushing seasonal streams with permanent snowfields gracing the rock walls above on both sides of the valley. At the pass, an old shelter cabin with a nearby stream makes a pleasant rest stop, with views of Lake Ellen Wilson and the cliffs surrounding it. Gunsight Pass is an outstanding place for close-range viewing of mountain goats in their natural environment.

From the pass, the trail descends the steep headwall of the Lincoln Creek valley, winding around the north wall of the cirque above Lake Ellen Wilson. Approximately 1.5 miles beyond the pass, a spur trail of .3 mile descends to the lake and its attendant campground. Overlooking the cooking area of the campground sits a huge *glacial erratic*, a boulder carried by a glacier and finally deposited when the glacier melted. The lake itself is excellent fishing for large and abundant brook trout.

From the Ellen Wilson spur, the trail begins climbing along the north wall of the cirque. As the trail nears Lincoln Pass (7,050 ft.), Lincoln Lake becomes visible in the valley to the south. As the trail swings onto a meadowy bench, the cliff ahead contains the outline of a horse and rider rising from its crest, above and to the east of a hole that pierces the cliff wall. The trail then swings around to the north, crossing a substantial stream that runs beneath rocky talus, before the final ascent to the pass. At this point, it is possible to skirt the cliff base to the west to get a complete view of Lake Ellen Wilson and Lincoln Lake, as well as 1,344-foot Beaver Chief Falls cascading down the rock face between them. Another .25 mile on the trail brings the hiker to Lincoln Pass, from which it is a short and easy climb to the summit of Lincoln Peak to the west.

As the trail descends from Lincoln Pass onto a high parkland shelf, it passes a small tarn which provides a refreshing dip to the trail-weary hiker (no soap, please). The trail descends along the shelf, passing the Sperry campground and entering the Sperry Chalets complex. The trail exits this complex in front of the dining hall, and descends .2 mile to the junction with the Sperry Glacier Overlook trail.

Sperry Glacier Overlook. The trail to Sperry Glacier is steep and challenging, rising 1,600 feet in 2.5 miles to Comeau Pass and then a little over a mile to the toe of the glacier. Hikers of this trail are rewarded with breathtaking vistas of the desolate Lewis Range peaks. The trail first ascends the headwall of a low cirque to the floor of a higher cirque, where the trail winds among rocky wastes interspersed with miniature meadows. Feather Woman and Akaiyan lakes form glassy reflecting pools for the cliffs to the south when these alpine lakes become free of ice in July. Beyond these two high tarns, the trail reaches the cirque's low headwall, which it passes through via a narrow stairway blasted into the living rock. Emerging from the top of this stairway, the hiker is greeted by awe-inspiring views of the mountaintops to the north and east, across the rock and snow wastes that stretch away toward

Sperry Glacier. By following rock cairns, it is possible to hike a mile further through this wasteland to the foot of Sperry Glacier, with its seasonal lakes at its base. An alpinist route exists connecting Sperry Glacier to the Hidden Lake trail (see Hidden Lake). Walking on the glacier is not recommended for hikers inexperienced in glacier travel.

From the Sperry Glacier spur trail, the Gunsight Pass trail descends steeply past Beaver Medicine Falls to the floor of the Sprague Creek valley, where it passes through dense stands of Douglas-fir inhabited by numerous mule deer. After following Sprague Creek for about three miles, the trail rounds the end of a spur ridge and crosses Snyder Creek. After this crossing, known as Crystal Ford, a trail to the east runs for 2.6 miles up a gentle valley to a campground at Snyder Lake, set among towering, snow-clad peaks. The main trail continues its descent down the Snyder Creek valley for 1.8 miles to the trail's terminus at Lake McDonald Lodge.

TRAIL 35 PIEGAN PASS see p.102 for map

General description: A day hike from Siyeh Bend to Piegan Pass, 4.5 mi. (7 km), or from Siyeh Bend to Many Glacier Hotel, 12.8 mi. (20.5 km)
Elevation gain: 1,670 ft.
Elevation loss: 2,640 ft.
Maximum elevation: 7,560 ft.
Difficulty: Moderate (south to north); strenuous (north to south)
Topo maps: Logan Pass, Many Glacier
Finding the trailhead: Siyeh Bend parking area, three miles east of Logan Pass on the Going-to-the-Sun Highway. Trail begins on the east bank of Siyeh Creek.

0.0   Trail sign.
1.2   Junction with Piegan Pass trail. Turn left for Piegan Pass.
2.7   Junction with Siyeh Pass trail. Stay left for Piegan Pass. The trail crosses a small creek and winds around the base of Cataract Mountain.
4.5   Piegan Pass. Trail descends steeply to Morning Eagle Falls.
7.7   Morning Eagle Falls.
8.7   Trail enters Grinnell complex at junction with Grinnell Lake trail. Stay right for fastest route to Many Glacier Hotel. Trail follows the foot of Allen Mtn.
10.5 Junction with Josephine Lake cutoff trail. Stay right for Many Glacier.
12.8 Many Glacier Hotel upper parking lot.

The trail: Piegan Pass links the St. Mary drainage with the popular Many Glacier area, through a high, barren col between Cataract Mountain and Mt. Pollock. There are no campgrounds along this route, so it must be attempted as a long day hike. The trail passes through a wide range of elevations, offering the hiker a diverse assemblage of ecological communities populated by a variety of wildlife species. Fantastic views are available all along the route, highlighted by a rarely seen view of the eastern face of the Garden Wall. Hikers may opt to detour to Grinnell Lake and continue around the north shore of Lake Josephine. This

Hiking toward Mt. Gould. Photo by Michael S. Sample.

option increases the length of the trip by approximately .5 mile and avoids trail sections heavily used by horse parties. The trail may also be hiked from north to south; this greatly increases its difficulty due to the low starting elevation.

The trail begins at Siyeh Bend on the Going-to-the-Sun Road, at a scenic crossing of Siyeh Creek. The open meadows and tiny fir trees are left behind quickly as the trail climbs onto well-drained slopes covered with tall spruce and fir trees. The trail switches

PIEGAN PASS

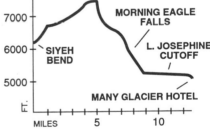

back as it climbs moderately through the trees, reaching a trail junction at mile 1.2. From this junction, the trail turns north, climbing gently through increasingly open forest interrupted by small patches of meadow. Going-to-the-Sun Mountain and Matahpi Peak loom to the east.

At mile 2.7, the trail reaches the Siyeh Pass junction among the open meadows of Preston Park. Looking to the west, the massive hump of Piegan Mountain is crowned by a large glacier bearing the same name, and 10,014-foot Mt. Siyeh blocks views to the north. Bearing left, the trail to Piegan Pass crosses a small creek and ascends onto the barren talus slopes of Cataract Mountain. The trail curves around to the head of the basin to reach the high col of Piegan Pass. The dark band of rock near the pass is an igneous intrusion that was laid down long after the older sedimentary strata. Mountain goats are frequently seen capering on rocky slopes and in grassy parklands around the pass, and marmots may be seen ambling along in rockslide areas.

Looking northward, the Bishop's Cap crowns the Garden Wall on the western rim of the valley, while Mt. Gould can be seen in the distance. Across the valley, the peak of Mt. Grinnell rises above the valley floor. The trail descends steeply to a high bench with subalpine fir parklands, and after crossing the gentle ledge, resumes a precipitous rate of descent. From the bench, the summit of Allen Mountain is easily seen to the northeast, owing its reddish hue to Grinnell argillite. After descending for about a quarter of a mile, the trail draws even with Morning Eagle Falls.

From this point, the trail follows Cataract Creek, crossing it twice on the way to the Feather Plume Cutoff 4.2 miles beyond the pass. Hikers wishing to see Grinnell Lake and avoid the horse trails should bear left at the cutoff trail (details provided under "The Grinnell Complex").

For hikers continuing directly to the hotel, the trail winds around the northwest flank of Allen Mountain, following the contours of the mountain. Below lies aquamarine Lake Josephine, which can be reached via several short cutoff trails along the route. Across the valley, the greenish base of Grinnell Point belies its Appekuny argillite nature. A sharp eye may spot the relatively fresh tailings from an abandoned mine below the tip of the point. Grizzly bears abound in the low-elevation meadows; care must be taken not to disturb these majestic creatures. The trail reaches its terminus at the upper parking lot of the Many Glacier Hotel. —*Candice Hanson*

TRAIL 36 *SIYEH PASS*

General description: A day hike from Siyeh Bend to Siyeh Pass, 4.7 mi. (7.5 km), or from Siyeh Bend to Sunrift Gorge exit, 10.3 mi. (16.5 km)
Elevation gain: 2,240 ft.
Elevation loss: 3,440 ft.
Maximum elevation: 8,080 ft.
Difficulty: Moderately strenuous
Topo maps: Logan Pass, Rising Sun
Finding the trailhead: Siyeh Bend, approximately three miles east of Logan Pass. Trail departs on the east bank of Siyeh Creek.

0.0   Trail sign. Trail ascends moderately along the west slope of Matahpi Peak.
1.2   Junction with Piegan Pass trail. Turn left for Siyeh Pass.
2.7   Junction with Siyeh Pass trail. Turn right for Siyeh Pass. Trail passes through Preston Park, past several glacial tarns, and then ascends moderately to Siyeh Pass.
4.7   Siyeh Pass. Trail ascends through a high saddle on Matahpi Peak.
5.6   Sexton Glacier overlook. Trail descends steeply, along the east wall of the Baring Creek valley.
10.0 Sunrift Gorge. Trail passes along the east rim of Sunrift Gorge.
10.3 Baring Creek exit.

The trail: Siyeh (pronounced Sigh-ee) Pass is a high elevation route that traverses two passes on its way around Going-to-the-Sun Mountain. Late snow accumulations often persist until late in the season on the south face of Matahpi

High saddle above Siyeh Pass.

Peak; rangers should be consulted concerning trail conditions before attempting this route.

The hike begins at Siyeh Bend, a large hairpin turn in the Going-to-the-Sun Road on the east side of the divide. The trail ascends from the east bank of Siyeh Creek onto the forested north flank of Going-to-the-Sun Mountain, through prime elk summer range. As the trail winds upward, it passes through stands of subalpine fir and spruce. At mile 2.7, the trail forks, with the left fork turning west to Piegan Pass and the right fork rising into Preston Park on its way to Siyeh Pass. The trail levels out, among beautiful fields of wildflowers

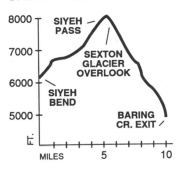

and stands of dwarfed fir and subalpine larch, with unnamed tarns on both sides. At the head of this small bowl, the trail climbs moderately to the barren saddle of Siyeh Pass. To the north lies Mt. Siyeh, overlooking Cracker Lake. A popular mountaineer's route ascends the south-facing slope above the pass and follows the spine of the ridge to the summit of Siyeh. Looking to the east, the Boulder Creek Valley frames pleasant vistas of the high plains.

From Siyeh Pass, the trail continues to climb, winding around the northeast slope of Matahpi Peak to a high, unnamed col. Views to the south encompass the ruddy summits across the St. Mary valley as well as peaks further south along the continental divide. As the trail descends into the Baring Valley, the Sexton Glacier can be clearly observed actively scraping away at the rock face across the valley. Terminal moraines, piles of grayish rock pushed up and deposited at the foot of the glacier, can be clearly seen on the near (north) side of the glacier's toe. The toe of the glacier overhangs a sheer drop-off on

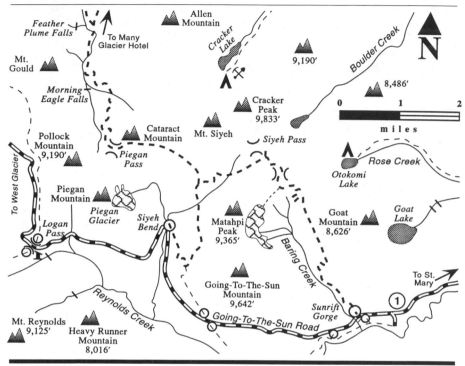

its south side, and huge chunks of ice occasionally break off and thunder down the cliff into the valley below.

As the trail descends to the extensive, grassy slopes on the valley's west wall, grizzly bears may be encountered, so appropriate caution should be displayed. The trail descends rather rapidly across many short switchbacks and winds through low, tortured stands of Douglas-fir toward the valley floor. The trail follows the east bank of Baring Creek as it cuts ever deeper into the rock strata, eventually forming Sunrift Gorge. The trail emerges onto the highway just below the foot of this chasm, at mile 40.

CONNECTING TRAILS

An administrative trail crosses from the Red Eagle trace to **Divide Creek**, over a low spur ridge of Curly Bear Mountain. The trail is poorly maintained and overrun with grizzly bears during the summer, and should be avoided. However, it provides a popular cross-country ski route in wintertime.

The **St. Mary Lake trail** begins in common with the Red Eagle trail, but splits off to the west at mile 5.1 of that trail, just before the second suspension bridge over Red Eagle Creek. The trail rounds the north flank of Red Eagle Mountain and follows the south shore of St. Mary Lake for ten miles, passing

Looking back at Mt. Reynolds over the flowery meadows of Preston Park. Photo by Candice Hanson.

below waterfalls created by tributary streams and offering views up the valley to the spine of the Continental Divide. After crossing the St. Mary River below St. Mary Falls, the trail forks. The east fork winds around the northwest shore of the lake for almost two miles past the Baring Creek junction to Going-to-the-Sun Point. The west fork follows the valley upward for 1.2 miles, linking up with the Gunsight Pass trail and a connecting trail to Siyeh and Piegan passes.

Grinnell Glacier trail. Photo by Michael S. Sample.

MANY GLACIER

Many Glacier Hotel was built in 1914 by the Great Northern Railway as a destination resort for its rail tourists. The hotel sits among soaring peaks and jagged aretes, which give this area the nickname "America's Little Switzerland." Since the park's creation, a myriad of trails have been built to reach the scenic wonders surrounding the hotel, making the Many Glacier area a hub for day-hiking activities. Lush meadows and tumbling waterfalls below snowy peaks invite the traveler to pause and contemplate the awe-inspiring beauty of the mountains.

The lower end of the valley is dominated by Lake Sherburne, which was impounded during the New Deal era. The formation of this reservoir inundated the old mining town of Altyn, which had once served as a center for unsuccessful gold and copper operations in the surrounding mountains.

The Many Glacier area is home to many kinds of wildlife. Most prominent is the majestic grizzly bear, which is frequently seen foraging for bulbs and berries on the open slopes of the surrounding mountains. Mountain goats cavort on the rocky ledges of sheer cliffs, and groups of bighorn sheep ewes with their young are sometimes seen in the lowlands around the hotel. The meadows and forests abound with rodents and songbirds of all kinds.

Visitor services are available in the area around the hotel as well as the nearby town of Babb, on the neighboring Blackfeet Indian Reservation. Trail rides of varying duration depart from the Many Glacier corral above the hotel, and a privately owned tour boat concession runs between the hotel and the upper end of Lake Josephine, providing interpretive tours and transportation to the upper Cataract Creek drainage. The spacious campground at Many Glacier provides sites for all types of vehicles, as well as a few sites reserved free-of-charge to backpackers on extended hikes through the area. The passes in the Many Glacier area access areas to the north, west, and south, providing the best opportunities for backpacking.

TRAIL 37 *CRACKER LAKE*

General description: A day hike or short backpack from Many Glacier Hotel to Cracker Lake campground, 6.1 mi. (10 km)
Elevation gain: 1,120 ft.
Maximum elevation: 5,900 ft.
Difficulty: Moderate
Topo maps: Many Glacier, L. Sherburne, Logan Pass
Finding the trailhead: Many Glacier trailhead, which is located at the south end of the upper parking lot for Many Glacier Hotel.

0.0   Trail sign. Trail winds around the base of Allen Mountain.
0.8   Trail follows Allen Creek.
1.3   Junction with Cracker Flats horse trail. Stay right for Cracker Lake.

Cracker Lake.

1.5	Trail crosses Allen Creek and ascends ridge between Allen and Canyon creeks.
2.5	Trail follows west bank of Canyon Creek, ascending moderately.
3.8	Trail crosses Canyon Creek.
5.6	Foot of Cracker Lake.
6.1	Cracker Lake campground.

The trail: Cracker Lake is a popular day hike destination for travelers in the Many Glacier area. The trail winds from the shore of Sherburne Reservoir up a forested ridgeline to a wide, meadowy basin filled with wildflowers and butterflies. Cracker Lake is a cold body of water made turquoise by light refraction through its load of suspended glacial silt. At the head of the lake, the old Cracker Mine lies beneath the towering cliff walls of Mt. Siyeh (Sigh'ee). There is also a small campground near the head of the lake for backpackers. This trail receives heavy horse traffic, so hikers should be prepared to yield to saddle stock when meeting on the trail.

CRACKER LAKE

TRAIL 37 *CRACKER LAKE*

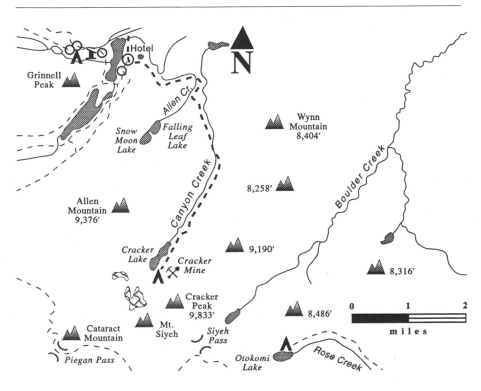

TRAIL 38 *THE GRINNELL COMPLEX*

General description: Day hikes from Swiftcurrent Picnic Area to Grinnell Glacier, 5.5 mi. (9 km); from Many Glacier Hotel to Grinnell Lake, 3.1 mi. (5 km); or from Josephine L. upper boat dock to Grinnell Lake, 0.9 mi. (1.5 km)
Topo map: Many Glacier

The trail: An extensive complex of interconnected trails originates near the Many Glacier Hotel and provides a variety of pleasant day hikes in the lower Cataract Creek valley. For a nominal fee, tour boats provide a guided cruise from the hotel to the upper end of Lake Josephine, also providing easy access to the upper end of the valley. The trails surrounding Lake Josephine provide open views of the high peaks at the head of the valley and provide fishermen's access to the low-elevation lakes on the valley floor. Trails from upper Lake Josephine pass through relict forests on their way to glittering waterfalls cascading from the valley's headwall. The Grinnell Glacier trail accesses one of the largest remaining glaciers in the park, and guided naturalist tours into the glacial cirque are offered at regular intervals. The Grinnell complex is covered in detail by trail number in the following pages. These trails are commonly closed due to the presence of bears; check with rangers before starting your trip. Horses are not permitted on these trails with the exception of #171, 113, 181, 172, 173, and 174 (between the Oastler Shelter and the Piegan Pass trail).

Swiftcurrent Lake Trail (trail #167)

The Swiftcurrent Lake trail is a well-traveled footpath and self-guiding nature trail that makes a complete circuit of this front-country lake, also providing access to hikers bound for points west in the valley. The trail begins at a picnic area .5 mile west of the hotel turnoff and immediately enters a stand of smallish lodgepole pines. Emerging from the trees, the trail crosses willow-choked Swiftcurrent Creek via a wooden bridge and reaches the wooded lakeshore shortly thereafter. After .7 mile, the trail reaches the upper Swiftcurrent boat dock, where trail #168 takes off to the west, around the north shore of Lake Josephine. Hikers bound for Grinnell Lake and Grinnell Glacier should take this trail.

The Swiftcurrent Lake trail continues its circuit of the lake, crossing Grinnell Creek. Immediately east of this crossing, a trail (#180) connects to the Josephine Lake south shore trail (#171). The main path continues around the lake, finally terminating at the hotel.

North Shore Lake Josephine (trail #168)

A paved footpath from the upper Swiftcurrent boat dock runs west to the foot of Lake Josephine, where it continues for 1.4 miles around the north shore of the lake as a dirt trail. The reddish summit of Allen Mountain dominates the skyline to the south. Midway up the lake, trail #170 to Grinnell Glacier climbs to the west. The trail continues to the head of the lake, where a cutoff trail climbs steeply to the Grinnell Glacier trail, and a connecting trail (#174) crosses the inlet via boardwalks to a trail junction at the Oastler Shelter.

TRAIL 38 *THE GRINNELL COMPLEX*

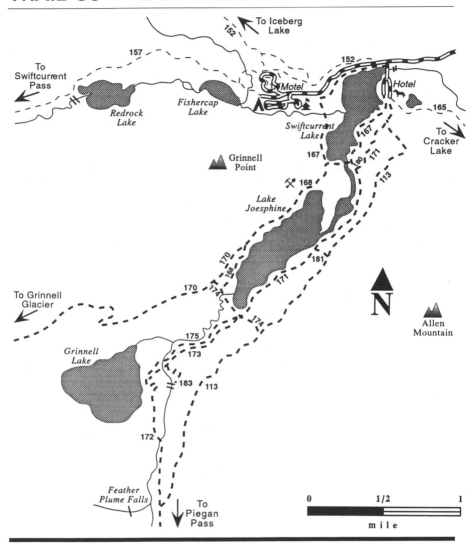

South Shore Lake Josephine (trail #171)

The first short section of the South Shore trail is heavily used by guided horse parties and provides a route from the hotel to the head of Lake Josephine. This trail has two origins: the southwest corner of the hotel's upper parking lot and the terminus of the hotel service road. The trail stays inland for .5 mile, descending to the valley floor shortly before reaching Stump Lake. At this point, trail #180 enters, connecting the south shore trail with the trail around Swiftcurrent Lake.

The trail winds around tiny Stump Lake, emerging at the eastern shore of Lake Josephine. Stunning views across the turquoise waters reveal Mt. Gould's

Mt. Gould and Angel Wing from above Lake Josephine.

blocky profile, with glaciers and snowbanks at its base. As the trail travels the length of the lake, Grinnell Point can be seen in profile above the north shore. Upon reaching the Oastler Shelter near the upper boat dock, this trail meets trails running to Piegan Pass and Grinnell Lake.

Grinnell Glacier Trail (trail #170)

Hikers accessing Upper Grinnell Lake and Grinnell Glacier start at the picnic area near Swiftcurrent Lake. The hiker skirts the western shore of Swiftcurrent Lake via trail #167 and then continues around Lake Josephine on trail #168.

Halfway up Lake Josephine, trail #170 rises through subalpine firs, above a relict forest spared by severe fires. The trail surmounts several steep switchbacks on the southern flank of Mt. Grinnell, emerging in alpine meadows high above the turquoise pool of Grinnell Lake and the waterfall at its head. As the trail gains altitude, panoramic views of the peaks crowding upper Cataract Creek can be seen to the south. The ruddy peak of Allen Mountain dominates the foreground, while Mt. Siyeh and Cataract Mountain loom above the head of the valley. The Garden Wall forms the western rim of the vale and rises to a massive peak overlooking the trail to the southwest—Mt. Gould.

The trail makes its way around steep cliffs above Grinnell Falls to a picnic area in a wooded glen. The picnic area offers log benches for the weary hiker and a pit toilet for those in search of other forms of relief. Shortly after leaving the picnic area, the hiker will ascend to a recent terminal moraine left by the retreating glacier.

From this point above the milky waters of Upper Grinnell Lake, one can see the fissures and ice caves of Grinnell Glacier. The long, narrow glacier above

GRINNELL GLACIER

7000 — GRINNELL GLACIER

6000 — GRINNELL GLACIER TRAIL JCT.

5000 — SWIFTCURRENT PICNIC AREA

FT.

MILES 5

The eastern side of the Garden Wall overshadowing lush parklands on the Grinnell Glacier trails. Photo by Candice Hanson.

and to the north, called "the Salamander," was connected with the main glacier until recent times. The tiny glacier high on the north shoulder of Mt. Gould is Gem Glacier, which is of great thickness. Upper Grinnell Lake, which lies at the foot of the glacier, derives its milky aquamarine color from the refraction of sunlight through suspended particles of fine dust created by the abrasive action of the glacier. Hikers inexperienced in the arts of glacier travel should not venture onto the ice; it is unstable and shot through with ice caves and fissures that pose a mortal threat to the unprepared.

Grinnell Lake Trails (#173 & #175)

Two trails, one open to horses and the other reserved for foot travel, leave the Oastler Shelter and run parallel for .8 mile to Grinnell Lake. The trails follow Cataract Creek through a relict forest for .5 mile before reaching a crossing at a suspension bridge. The main trail crosses the creek, while a spur trail (#183) switchbacks up the creek's eastern shore to Hidden Falls. Horses are not permitted on this trail.

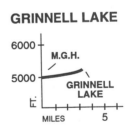

The primary trail continues west, reaching Grinnell Lake after another .3 mile. The lake sits at the foot of a reddish cliff, down which Grinnell Falls cascades from its source in the glacier above. The graceful promontory that extends from the eastern flank of Mt. Gould to overshadow the lake's southern shore is known as Angel Wing. Trail #172 continues south from the lake, passing Feather Plume Falls on its way to meet the Piegan Pass trail.

Feather Plume Cutoff (trail #172)

The Feather Plume Cutoff trail provides a link between the Piegan Pass trail and the upper Grinnell Complex. From Grinnell Lake, the trail climbs briskly below the eastern wall of Angel Wing, the smallish promontory projecting from the eastern face of Mt. Gould. The trail continues south, crossing Cataract Creek to its eastern shore. Shortly after passing below the misty base of Feather Plume Falls, the trail reaches its terminus at the Piegan Pass trail junction.

Piegan Pass (trail #113)

The Piegan Pass trail begins at the upper parking lot at the hotel and follows the contours of Mt. Allen as it skirts above the south shore of Lake Josephine. Connecting trails provide links to Lake Josephine some 1.2 (trail #181) and 2.3 (trail #174) miles from the hotel. The trail then bends to the south and joins the Feather Plume Cutoff trail about 4.1 miles from the hotel. A complete description of the Piegan Pass trail is provided under "Trails from the St. Mary Valley." —Candice Hanson

TRAIL 39 SWIFTCURRENT PASS

General description: A day hike or extended backpack from Swiftcurrent Inn to Swiftcurrent Pass, 6.6 mi. (10.5 km), or from Swiftcurrent Inn to Granite Park, 7.6 mi. (12 km)
Elevation gain: 2,225 ft.
Elevation loss: 735 ft.
Maximum elevation: 6,770 ft.
Difficulty: Strenuous
Topo maps: Many Glacier, Ahern Pass
Finding the trailhead: Trail begins at the west end of the Swiftcurrent Lodge coffee shop parking lot.

0.0	Trail sign.
0.2	Junction with horse trail. Stay left for Swiftcurrent Pass. Trail follows floor of Swiftcurrent valley, climbing gently.
2.0	Redrock Lake.
3.3	Bullhead Lake.
3.5	Trail begins ascent to Swiftcurrent Pass.
6.6	Swiftcurrent Pass.
6.7	Swiftcurrent Lookout trail junction. Trail descends gently to Granite Park.
7.6	Granite Park Chalet.

The trail: The Swiftcurrent Pass trail follows the Swiftcurrent valley past a chain of lakes to a steep ascent of the Continental Divide. This ascent to the pass is quite strenuous, and the trail is much easier if taken from west to east. It may be attempted as a strenuous day hike, or plugged into a more extended itinerary by linking up with the Highline trail.

The trail begins at the Swiftcurrent Motor Lodge and winds westward along the valley floor, among groves of tall aspen interspersed with lodgepole pine. The trail passes to the north of Fishercap Lake, which can only be glimpsed briefly through a few holes in the vegetation. The trail climbs gently, crossing

Looking down on Bullhead Lake.

a small stream on its way to Redrock Lake. Notice that harsh growing conditions have stunted the pines and aspens around the lake. The trail continues west, passing Redrock Falls above the head of the lake. Two miles beyond Redrock Lake, the trail reaches Bullhead Lake, from which a northward glance reveals Mt. Wilbur, Iceberg Peak, and the North Swiftcurrent Glacier on the east face of Swiftcurrent Mountain.

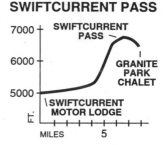

SWIFTCURRENT PASS

After Bullhead Lake, the trees fall away entirely, giving way to grassy fields. The trail reaches the towering headwall of the valley, and begins a steep ascent beside precipitous waterfalls that issue forth from the Swiftcurrent Glacier high above. The trail crisscrosses cliff faces on its way to the pass, affording spectacular views of the chain of lakes in the valley below. As the trail emerges above the cliff face, it climbs through miniature meadows on its way to the low saddle of Swiftcurrent Pass.

Shortly beyond the pass, a side trail takes off to the north to ascend across steep switchbacks some 1.4 miles to Swiftcurrent Lookout. The view from the lookout is outstanding, with a glacier-carved rockscape sweeping away in all directions. The main trail descends gently for .9 mile to Granite Park, where it joins the Highline trail.

TRAIL 39 and 40 *SWIFTCURRENT PASS, ICEBERG LAKE*

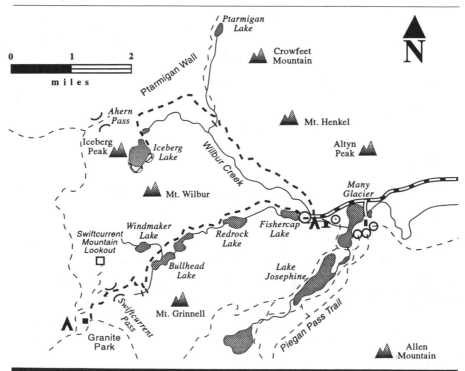

TRAIL 40 *ICEBERG LAKE*

General description: A day hike from Swiftcurrent Inn to Iceberg Lake, 4.5 mi. (7 km)
Elevation gain: 1,194 ft.
Maximum elevation: 6,100 ft.
Difficulty: Moderate
Topo map: Many Glacier
Finding the trailhead: Iceberg-Ptarmigan trailhead, which departs from the north end of the Swiftcurrent Motor Lodge complex, among the cabins behind the coffee shop. A parking pullout at the trailhead is marked with a trailhead sign.

0.0 Trail sign.
0.1 Junction with trail #167. Turn left for Iceberg Lake.
2.3 Trail crosses Ptarmigan Creek at Ptarmigan Falls.
2.4 Junction with Ptarmigan Tunnel trail. Stay left for Iceberg Lake.
4.4 Trail crosses Iceberg Creek below an unnamed tarn.
4.5 Iceberg Lake.

The trail: Iceberg Lake is a striking, aquamarine tarn, which is surrounded on three sides by towering cliffs. Ice-out may not occur until mid-July, and bergs for which the lake was named may be seen floating about well after that date. This stunning destination, as well as the brilliant wildflowers along the route, make the Iceberg Lake trail one of the most popular hikes in the park. It crosses fine grizzly bear habitat, and bears are frequently seen on the open slopes on both sides of the trail.

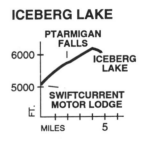

The hike begins at a short connecting trail that climbs briskly for several hundred yards to join the main trail coming in from the hotel. The trail then turns northwest, climbing gently along the open south slopes high above Wilbur Creek. Look for the magenta spikes of fireweed and the bulblike inflorescences of beargrass (a member of the lily family) early in the season. The trail passes below Altyn Peak, a greenish massif of Appekuny argillite, and Mt. Wilbur, known to the Blackfeet as "Heavy Shield Mountain," rises across the valley to the south. The trail passes into open forests on its way to Ptarmigan Falls, a popular rest stop on hot summer days.

Shortly after passing the falls, the trail reaches the junction with the Ptarmigan Tunnel trail, and then turns southwest along the Ptarmigan Wall through increasingly alpine scenery toward the head of the valley. Looking south, a waterfall on Iceberg Creek can be glimpsed through the trees. The trail climbs gently as it curls around to the south into the glacial cirque that holds the lake.

The 3,000-foot cliffs surrounding the lake provide prime escape habitat for mountain goats, which are frequently seen in this area. Talus slopes along the lake's south shore are home to a variety of small mammals, including pikas

Hiker at Iceberg Lake.

and ground squirrels. The permanent snowfields at the head of the lake are remnants of a glacier that until recently occupied the basin beneath the cool shadows of Iceberg Peak.

TRAIL 41 *PTARMIGAN TUNNEL* see p. 120 for map

General description: A day hike or backpack from Swiftcurrent Inn to Ptarmigan Tunnel, 5.0 mi. (8 km), or from Swiftcurrent Inn to Elizabeth Lake foot, 9.8 mi. (16 km)
Elevation gain: 2,480 ft.
Elevation loss: 2,518 ft.
Maximum elevation: 7,200 ft.
Difficulty: Moderately strenuous
Topo maps: Many Glacier, Gable Mtn.
Finding the trailhead: Iceberg-Ptarmigan trailhead, located at the north end of the Swiftcurrent Motor Lodge complex, among the cabins behind the coffee shop.

0.0 Trail sign.
0.1 Junction with Iceberg Lake trail. Turn left for Ptarmigan Tunnel.
2.4 Trail crosses Ptarmigan Creek at Ptarmigan Falls.
2.5 Junction with Ptarmigan Tunnel trail. Turn right for Ptarmigan Tunnel.
4.1 Ptarmigan Lake. Trail ascends steeply to the tunnel.
5.0 Ptarmigan Tunnel. Trail begins descent into Belly River valley.
5.4 Best view of Mt. Merritt to the north.
7.8 Junction with Redgap Pass trail. Stay left for Elizabeth Lake.
9.8 Elizabeth Lake.

The trail: The spectacular views and only moderate difficulty of the Ptarmigan Tunnel trail make it a preferred route among local hikers accessing the Belly River drainage. The trail passes from Swiftcurrent Lodge up the Wilbur Creek valley, turning northward past Ptarmigan Lake. High above the lake, the trail passes through a knife-edge ridge and descends to the foot of Elizabeth Lake, after covering a distance of 9.8 miles. The Ptarmigan Tunnel itself may be a day-hike destination from the Many Glacier area as

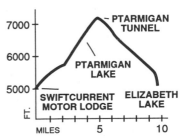

PTARMIGAN TUNNEL

well as an access point to the Belly River country. The tunnel is subject to seasonal closures due to snowdrifts and occasional grizzly bear presence; check at the Many Glacier ranger station for trail status.

The route to the Ptarmigan Tunnel begins at Swiftcurrent Lodge and follows the Iceberg Lake trail around the south slopes of Altyn Peak to a trail junction at mile 2.5. At this point, the trail to Ptarmigan Tunnel takes off to the north, ascending through open woodlands to the foot of Ptarmigan Lake, which lies in a gravelly, barren-looking cirque below the tunnel. After a short but

Mt. Merritt and Natoas Peak, beyond Ptarmigan Tunnel.

challenging ascent, the trail reaches the tunnel, which was blasted through the solid rock of the Ptarmigan Wall in 1931. Looking southward from inside the tunnel, Mt. Wilbur is framed by the massive steel doors of the tunnel. After emerging from the north side of the tunnel, you will see Elizabeth Lake in the valley below, with Natoas Peak rising above it.

The best views on the entire trail are only half a mile north of the tunnel, around the east wall of the barren cirque below. From this viewpoint, the twisted spires of Mt. Merritt can be seen rising above the Old Sun Glacier, and to the southwest, Helen Lake can be seen nestled at the foot of Ipasha Peak.

The trail continues its descent among stands of twisted white-bark pines to a junction with the Redgap Pass trail some 2.4 miles beyond the tunnel. From this junction, it's only two miles of descent through mixed forests to a suspension bridge that crosses the Belly River into the Elizabeth Lake (foot) campground. The campground overlooks the fish-laden lake, with views of the cockscomb of the Ptarmigan Wall, through which the hiker has just passed.

TRAIL 42 *POIA LAKE-REDGAP PASS*

General description: A day hike or backpack from Many Glacier Road to Poia Lake, 6.4 mi. (10.5 km); from Many Glacier Road to Redgap Pass, 12.0 mi. (19 km); or from Many Glacier Road to Elizabeth Lake foot, 16.6 mi. (26.5 km)

Elevation gain to Poia Lake: 1,350 ft.
Elevation loss to Poia Lake: 415 ft.
Elevation gain to Elizabeth Lake: 3,115 ft.
Elevation loss to Elizabeth Lake: 3,133 ft.
Maximum elevation: 7,520 ft. (Redgap Pass)
Difficulty: Moderate (Poia L.); strenuous (Redgap Pass)
Topo maps: L. Sherburne, Many Glacier, Gable Mtn.
Finding the trailhead: Trailhead parking lot approximately three miles west of Entrance Station, and .25 mile east of Apikuni Falls trailhead, on north side of Many Glacier Road.

0.0   Trail sign.
3.3   Junction with Sherburne cutoff trail. Stay left for Poia Lake. Trail winds below Apikuni Mtn. and ascends Swiftcurrent Ridge.
3.6   Swiftcurrent Ridge Lake. Trail begins descent into Kennedy Creek valley.
4.9   Trail reaches Kennedy Creek and begins ascent to Poia L.
6.4   Poia Lake campground. Trail ascends gently along the Kennedy valley floor.
9.4   Trail begins ascent toward Redgap Pass.
12.0 Redgap Pass. Trail begins steep descent to Elizabeth Lake.
14.6 Junction with Ptarmigan Tunnel trail. Turn right for Elizabeth Lake.
16.6 Elizabeth Lake (foot) campground.

The trail: The Redgap Pass trail offers a long, arduous route through the desolate Kennedy Creek valley to the Belly River country to the north. Many backpackers opt for Poia Lake as a short-range backpack.

The trail begins at the Many Glacier Road, not far from the Apikuni Falls trailhead. The trail ascends as it winds eastward beneath

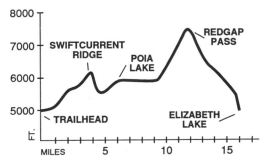

POIA LAKE-REDGAP PASS

the gabled south face of Apikuni Mountain. Sherburne Reservoir is visible in the valley below. After three miles, the trail mounts a wooded ridgeline, where it meets an insanely steep one-mile cutoff trail from the Entrance Station coming in from the south. A few hundred yards beyond this junction, the trail passes the west shore of Swiftcurrent Ridge Lake, a marshy mere set in the deep forest of the crest of the ridge.

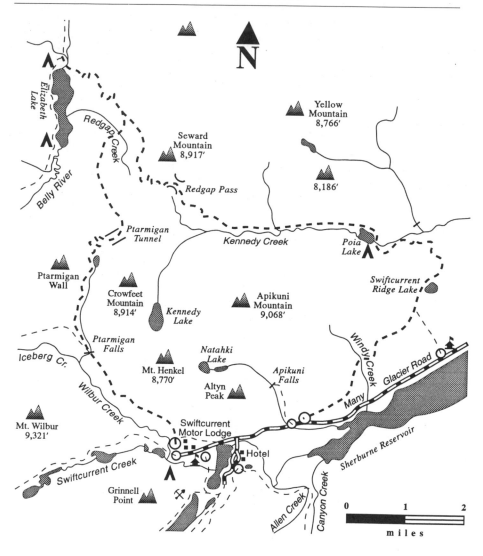

From this lake, the trail drops into the Kennedy Creek valley to the north, descending through forests interrupted by small pockets of open marsh. Upon reaching the valley floor, the trail crosses a series of beaver ponds set among large aspens and turns west along the south bank of the creek. The Altyn limestone mass of Yellow Mountain rises to the north, with a pleasant waterfall nestled at its base, as the trail winds its way upward for a mile and a half through gravelly rock gardens to Poia Lake. The lake was named for a half-mortal in Blackfeet legend named "Star Boy" who saved the life of Morning

Unnamed tarn and peak below Redgap Pass.

Star and thus restored the people to Sun Chief's favor. The campground sits on a wooded knoll at the foot of the lake, looking westward toward the moors above the lake. The lake is deep and cold and is surrounded by blocky cliffs on both sides, but contains no fish.

The trail crosses the outlet of the lake and skirts its north shore on the way to Redgap Pass. From the head of the lake, the trail winds for three miles through open muskeg and wooded valley floor before ascending steeply toward the pass. As the trail passes out of white-bark and lodgepole pine forests into open subalpine fir parkland, beargrass blossoms dot the slopes on all sides. A backward glance reveals the hulking mass of Apikuni Mountain to the south, and Mt. Henkel and Crowfeet Mountain crowd the head of the valley, with Kennedy Lake at their feet. As it reaches the windswept pass, the trail passes immediately beneath a towering chimney of reddish Grinnell argillite. Upon cresting the rise, the backpacker is greeted with stunning views of Old Sun Glacier lying at the base of the towering spires of Mt. Merritt.

The trail then drops into a high, treeless cirque and winds around the west face of a rocky knob onto a series of high benches. Descending through ragged stands of pine, the trail makes is way to a junction with the Ptarmigan Tunnel trail. From this point, it is a foot-pounding two-mile descent to the foot of Elizabeth Lake.

Cracker Flats. A horse trail runs from the Cracker Lake trail for .5 mile to Cracker Flats along the shore of Lake Sherburne. These flats are the former site of the mining town of Altyn, inundated by the formation of the reservoir. A trail once ran from the flats through forested slopes to the crest of Boulder Ridge five miles to the east, but this trail has disappeared through long years of disuse.

Apikuni Falls. A short, well-maintained trail runs for one mile to Apikuni Falls from mile 10.4 of the Many Glacier Road. The high cirque beyond is accessible to climbers via a little scrambling. The enterprising bushwhacker who reaches the head of this tiny bowl is rewarded views of Natahki Lake and the towering cliff walls surrounding it.

Kennedy Creek. A primitive route once ran up Kennedy Creek from a maze of jeep trails outside the park, linking up with the Poia-Redgap trail. No trace of this trail remains, and hikers planning to use this route should forget about following the old trail and hike up the creek bed instead.

THE BELLY RIVER COUNTRY

The valley of the Belly River is one of the most untamed and beautiful areas left in North America. It is accessible only by trail, and its remoteness makes it a backpacker's paradise. Chief Mountain stands as a lone sentinel over the northern plains, an island of ancient limestone spared by the erosive glaciers that once surrounded it. The rugged peaks of the inner ranges are dominated by the massive pinnacles of Mt. Merritt, which sports three glaciers on its flanks.

Place names reflect the importance of this area to Native Americans: Atsina Lake, Mokowanis Creek, Gros Ventre Falls, and the Belly River itself are named after the Gros Ventre or "Big Belly" tribe of the northern plains, Kaina Creek was named for a northern band of Blackfeet that reside in Canada, and the Stoney Indians of the Canadian Rockies left their name on the pass and peak at the head of Mokowanis Creek.

The streams and lakes draining toward Hudson Bay abound with fish, including rainbow and brook trout, mountain whitefish, and the arctic grayling. The latter is limited to only a few areas in Montana, including Elizabeth Lake and the Belly River. The grassy meadows of the valley floor provide forage for abundant elk, who share the valley with deer, mountain lions, and many other species of wildlife. The surrounding ridges are covered with a mixture of spruce and lodgepole pines on the well-drained sites, with quaking aspen groves occupying spring and seep areas.

The Belly River valley can be accessed from the Chief Mountain Highway, or over passes from Goat Haunt R.S. on Waterton Lake or the Many Glacier area. Trails tend to take their time in getting places, and thus this area offers few opportunities for day hikers. The closest ranger stations from which permits are available are at Many Glacier and St. Mary. In addition, there is a ranger station near the confluence of the Mokowanis and Belly rivers, which is manned from May through September. Don't go into the area without a permit.

TRAIL 43 *THE BELLY RIVER TRAIL*

General description: A backpack from Chief Mtn. Customs to Belly River R.S., 6.1 mi. (10 km); from Chief Mtn. Customs to Elizabeth L. (foot), 9.3 mi. (15 km); or from Chief Mtn. Customs to Helen Lake, 13.6 mi. (22 km)
Elevation loss: 744 ft.
Elevation gain: 492 ft.
Maximum elevation: 5,329 ft.
Difficulty: Moderate
Topo maps: Gable Mtn., Many Glacier
Finding the trailhead: Chief Mountain Customs trailhead, located on Montana State Highway 17, within sight of the Border Patrol buildings.

0.0   Trail sign. Trail descends steeply into the Belly River valley.
2.0   Trail reaches the valley floor and turns southwest.

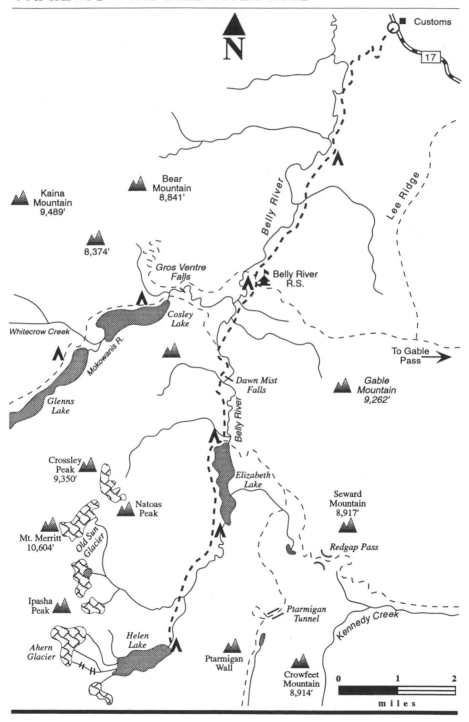

Customs

17

Kaina
Mountain
9,489'

Bear
Mountain
8,841'

8,374'

Belly River

Lee Ridge

Gros Ventre
Falls

Belly River
R.S.

Whitecrow Creek

Cosley
Lake

Mokowanis R.

Glenns
Lake

Dawn Mist
Falls

Belly River

To Gable
Pass

Gable
Mountain
9,262'

Crossley
Peak
9,350'

Natoas
Peak

Elizabeth
Lake

Seward
Mountain
8,917'

Mt. Merritt
10,604'

Old Sun
Glacier

Redgap Pass

Ipasha
Peak

Ptarmigan
Tunnel

Kennedy Creek

Ahern
Glacier

Helen
Lake

Ptarmigan
Wall

Crowfeet
Mountain
8,914'

0   1   2

m i l e s

3.0   3-mile campground.

6.0   Junction with Stoney Indian Pass. Stay left for Elizabeth Lake.

6.1   Belly River Ranger Station. Junction with Gable Pass trail. Keep right for Elizabeth Lake.

6.3   Belly River campground located next to river below fenced paddock. Trail ascends wooded valley and crosses Belly River to north bank.

7.6   Junction with Cosley Lake cutoff trail. Stay left for Elizabeth Lake.

8.1   Dawn Mist Falls.

9.3   Elizabeth Lake (foot) campground. Ptarmigan-Redgap trail enters behind horse hitching post. Bear right to lake head and Helen Lake. Trail follows west shore of Elizabeth Lake.

10.9   Elizabeth Lake (head) campground. Trail continues south, climbing gradually. Trail crosses outlet of Helen Lake before reaching campground on the eastern shore.

13.6   Helen Lake campground.

The trail: The Belly River trail provides low-elevation access to some of the most beautiful country in Glacier National Park. The valley floor is clear of snow as early as mid-May, making this trail a good choice for early-season access to rugged country.

THE BELLY RIVER TRAIL

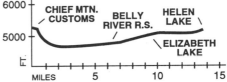

The trail begins at the Chief Mountain customs, on a ridge overlooking the Belly River valley. It immediately enters a dense stand of lodgepole pines on the ridgetop before descending steeply down the ridge face. The trail passes many springs populated by aspen stands, whose white trunks contrast sharply with their bright green foliage. Aspens reproduce most frequently by sending out shoots from existing roots (as opposed to seeds), and thus a thicket of aspen trees most likely represents a collection of clones of the original parent plant.

When the trail reaches the valley floor, it turns south, following the gentle grade of the Belly River through grassy meadows and stands of pine and aspen. At mile three, the trail enters the Three-mile campground, which is located next to the river in a small stand of conifers. This campground is a popular lunch spot for both hikers and biting flies. An old trail once crossed the river at the campground, winding around the base of Sentinel Mountain into the North Fork of the Belly River, but this trail is not maintained regularly. From this area, Bear and Sentinel mountains can be seen to the west, while the monumental mass of Chief Mountain rises to the east.

The trail continues up the valley to the Belly River Ranger Station, where trails from Gable Pass and the Mokowanis River valley converge with the Belly River trail. The meadow in front of this historic station provides a view up the Mokowanis Valley, and elk can often be seen feeding in the horse paddock at dusk. The Belly River campground is located on a spur trail that descends to the river from the far side of the meadow and is pleasantly situated among large spruce trees. The ice-cold, clear Belly River does contain grayling and rainbow trout but is generally considered poor fishing.

From the Belly River Ranger Station, the trail ascends through dense lodgepole pine forest and crosses the river via a suspension bridge before arriving at a short spur which leads to Dawn Mist Falls. This torrential waterfall cascades over the hard rock of the Lewis overthrust sill, which extends over several strata of softer rock.

From this point, it is a mile further to the foot of beautiful Elizabeth Lake, which provides excellent fishing for grayling and rainbow trout in the one- to two-pound class. Across the lake, the jagged arete of the Ptarmigan Wall dominates the landscape, and in early spring, frequent avalanches can be seen cascading down its west face. The lake itself is a deep aquamarine color, as a result of glacial flour suspended in the water column.

The trail winds around the eastern shore of the lake, providing excellent views of the reddish summit of Seward Mountain. At the head of the lake is a smaller, poorly developed campsite. Leaving the lake, the trail continues southward through dense vegetation and past an occasional beaver pond. After crossing a substantial creek, hikers can see glacier-clad Mount Merritt framed by the steep valley to the west. As the trail continues southward, it crosses several low lateral moraine hills, finally emerging into subalpine fir parkland and crossing the Belly River at the outlet of Helen Lake.

Helen Lake is a desolate, barren body of water situated below the cliffs of Ipasha and Ahern peaks. The upper part of the Ahern Glacier can be seen in the saddle between these two peaks. The campground at Helen Lake is a dispersed-use area in a meadow next to the lake, with a cooking area further inland among the trees.

TRAIL 44 *MOKOWANIS RIVER-STONEY INDIAN PASS*

General description: A backpack from Chief Mtn. Customs to Cosley Lake campground, 8.8 mi. (14 km); from Chief Mtn. Customs to Stoney Indian Pass, 17.9 mi. (29 km); or from Chief Mtn. Customs to Goat Haunt R.S., 26.4 mi. (42.5 km)
Elevation gain: 2,725 ft.
Elevation loss: 3,869 ft.
Maximum elevation: 6,908 ft.
Difficulty: Moderate (to Upper Glenns L.); moderately strenuous (to Goat Haunt)
Topo maps: Gable Mtn., Mt. Cleveland, Ahern Pass, Porcupine Ridge
Finding the trailhead: Chief Mountain Customs trailhead, on Montana State Highway 17 within sight of the border facilities, or Goat Haunt Ranger Station, reached by ferry or trail from Waterton (Alberta) township.

0.0   Trail sign. Trail descends steeply to the Belly River valley.
2.0   Trail reaches the valley floor and turns southwest.
3.0   Three-mile campground.
6.0   Junction with Stoney Indian Pass trail, just before Belly River R.S. Turn right for Stoney Indian Pass. Trail crosses Belly River and ascends a finger ridge westward.
7.9   Gros Ventre Falls.

Backpacking toward Stoney Indian Peaks. Photo by Michael S. Sample.

8.0 Junction with Bear Mtn. Overlook trail (1.7 mi., strenuous). Stay left for Stoney Indian Pass.

8.2 Junction with Belly River cutoff trail at foot of Cosley Lake. Stay right for Stoney Indian Pass.

8.7 Spur trail to Cosley Lake campground. Trail follows north shore of Cosley L., then crosses Whitecrow Creek.

10.2 Glenns Lake (foot) campground. Trail follows north shore of Glenns Lake.

12.8 Upper Glenns campground.

13.1 Junction with Mokowanis Lake trail (1.3 mi., easy). Stay right for Stoney Indian Pass.

13.2 Mokowanis Junction campground. Trail climbs moderately, following Mokowanis River.

15.9 Atsina Lake. Trail climbs steeply, flattens out, then begins steep ascent of pass.

17.9 Stoney Indian Pass. Trail descends steeply.

18.9 Stoney Indian Lake campground. Trail descends fairly steeply.

21.5 Junction with Waterton Valley trail. Turn right for Goat Haunt.

23.9 Junction with Kootenai Lake spur trail. Stay right for Goat Haunt.

26.4 Goat Haunt R.S.

MOKOWANIS RIVER-STONEY INDIAN PASS

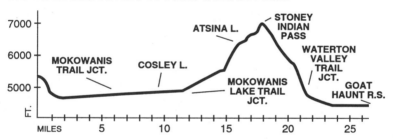

The trail: The trail to Stoney Indian Pass begins in common with the Belly River trail, which it follows for six miles before splitting off to the north at the Belly River Ranger Station. A detailed description of this section is listed under **Belly River Trail.**

From the Belly River Ranger Station, the trail turns west, descending gently to the river, which is crossed via a suspension bridge. The trail then ascends onto a thin ridgetop covered in lodgepole pines and beargrass, where numerous butterflies may be seen on sunny days. As the trail traverses the slopes above the Mokowanis River, a short spur to the left passes above Gros Ventre Falls, a roaring cataract that plunges over 100 feet.

Shortly before reaching Cosley Lake, the trail reaches a junction with the Bear Mountain overlook trail. This trail winds steeply 1.7 miles to an old lookout site, high on the southwest flank of Bear Mountain. From various points on the trail, the Whitecrow Glacier can be seen at the base of Mt. Cleveland, the tallest peak in the park. A spur peak projects from the eastern side of this mountain, appearing isolated from the rest of the range by a trick of perspective.

Just beyond the Overlook trail junction, the main trail reaches the foot of

Mokowanis Lake.

Cosley Lake. Following the northern shore, the trail reaches a cutoff trail to a campground about one-third of the way up the lake. After this junction, the trail continues along the lakeshore, among stands of large pines. Above the head of the lake, the trail crosses rushing Whitecrow Creek. The delta formed by silt deposited by this creek completely dammed the Mokowanis River, forming Glenns Lake above it. The trail continues up the western shore of Glenns Lake, which is 2.8 miles long. There are two campgrounds along the shore of the lake, at the foot and the head. Across this lake, the tall summit of Mt. Merritt rises at the western end of Crossley Ridge. The symmetrical form of Pyramid Peak graces the head of the valley.

At the head of Glenns Lake, a trail to Mokowanis Lake enters from the south. This trail is only one mile long, and the extra detour is well worth the effort. The trail crosses the inlet to Glenns Lake below White Quiver Falls, a delicate skein of lacy water that flows down the surface of a tilted stratum of rock. The trail then climbs briefly through pine forest and across naked rock to the foot of Mokowanis Lake. This lake lies at the base of a natural amphitheater surrounded by soaring pinnacles. A large waterfall which descends from Margaret Lake is visible above the head of the lake. There is a campground located at the head of this lake, on the eastern shore.

Immediately after the Mokowanis trail junction, the trail arrives at a campground on the main river. The trail ascends the forested valley floor, then climbs rather steeply past several falls on its way to Atsina Lake. The trail crosses the inlet stream and surmounts the headwall above the lake, passing near a pair of twin cascades: Paiota Falls is the closer; Atsina Falls the more distant. As the trail gains altitude, fantastic views open up on all sides. To the south, Mt. Kipp rises above Raven Quiver Falls. The Shepard Glacier enrobes the eastern flank of Cathedral Peak which rises ahead.

The trail climbs quickly into a small basin occupied by a small tarn, among

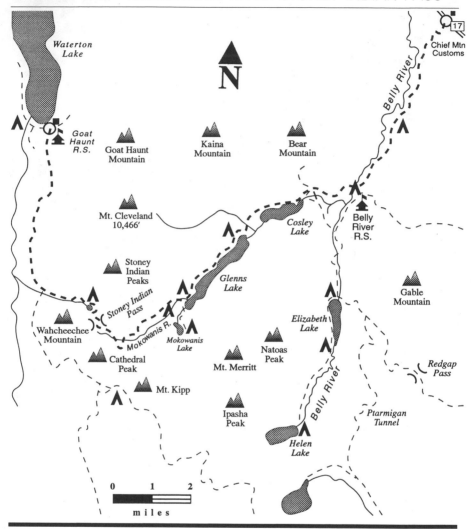

charming alpine parklands. Above the tarn, the trail climbs steeply to the high, bare col of Stoney Indian Pass. The Stoney Indians were a small band related to the Assiniboine which inhabited the Belly River country. From the pass, the Stoney Indian Peaks dominate the skyline to the north, and Wahcheechee Mountain overlooks the pass to the west.

The trail descends steeply across many switchbacks to the treeless valley below, occupied by Stoney Indian Lake. There is a campground at the outlet of this high alpine tarn. Below the lake, the trail continues a fairly steep descent past some falls to the floor of the Waterton Valley. Here, the Stoney Indian trail joins the Waterton Valley trail, which descends gently for 4.9 miles to Goat Haunt Ranger Station (see separate listing under The Highline and the Waterton Lake Vicinity).

TRAIL 45 *SLIDE LAKE-GABLE PASS*

General description: A backpack from Montana Highway 17 to Slide Lake, 8.6 mi. (14 km); from Montana Highway 17 to Gable Pass, 10.6 mi. (17 km); or from Montana Highway 17 to Belly River R.S., 13.2 mi. (21 km)
Elevation gain: 2,100 ft.
Elevation loss: 3,300 ft.
Maximum elevation: 7,220 ft.
Difficulty: Moderate
Topo maps: Chief Mtn., Gable Mtn.
Finding the trailhead: Otatso Creek Road, an unmarked primitive road with a cattle guard and barbed-wire fence gate across it, approximately .3 mile southeast of the Chief Mountain overlook on Montana State Highway 17. For a skilled driver, the road is passable to all vehicles for two miles, to the second cattle guard. After that, the road gets steep and gullied, and there is a spring in the road about one mile further that has a reputation for swallowing four-wheel-drive vehicles whole. If by some luck a driver can pass this mudhole, the road is fairly passable until it is entirely washed out one mile before the park boundary.

0.0 Barbed-wire gate at State Highway 17. Please remember to close gate. Primitive road follows top of Sandy Ridge.
2.0 Cattle guard. Road begins moderate descent to Otatso Creek valley.
6.0 Road washout.
7.0 Park boundary.
7.2 Old Otatso Creek patrol cabins.
8.4 Slide Lake campground.
8.6 Slide Lake. Junction with Gable Pass trail. Turn right for Gable Pass. Trail ascends, crossing benches.
10.2 Trail crosses boulderfield and continues moderate climb to Gable Pass.
10.6 Gable Pass. Trail winds westward, descending along the flanks of Gable Mtn.
10.9 Junction with Lee Ridge trail. Stay left for Belly River R.S.
13.2 Belly River R.S.

The trail: Slide Lake is seldom visited except by wily Canadians and Blackfeet who fish its population of large bull trout. The lake is situated in a glacial valley, surrounded by desolate peaks and wind-blown parkland. Access is provided by an unimproved jeep trail which crosses the last rolling ridges of the high plains, among meadows and aspen stands, before descending into the Otatso Creek valley. This track

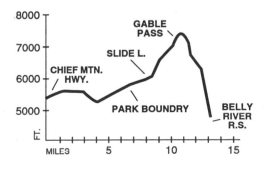

SLIDE LAKE-GABLE PASS

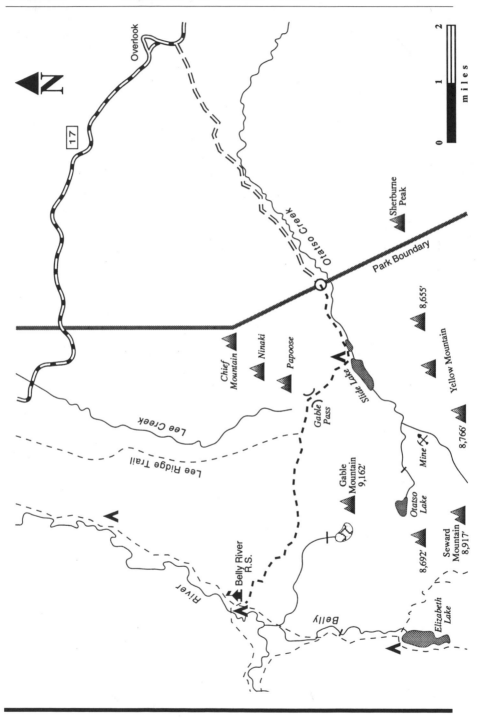

Slide Lake.

passes immediately to the south of Chief Mountain, sacred to the Blackfeet tribe, providing seldom-seen views of the mountain's south face. The blocklike form of this solitary monument has long provided a landmark for travelers of the northern plains. To the west, along the same ridge, rise the twisted spires of Ninaki (Squaw) and Papoose peaks.

As the dirt track enters the park and becomes a trail, it passes a small complex of dilapidated patrol cabins. The trail then winds up through parklike benches, following the rushing rivulet of Otatso Creek. As the trail ascends into a clearing, it passes along the north shore of a small, unnamed tarn at the base of Yellow Mountain. This tarn and the larger body of Slide Lake above it were formed when landslides from the flanks of Yellow Mountain blocked the flow of Otatso Creek, forming natural dams. The Slide Lake campground is situated above the upper end of the unnamed tarn and consists of a couple of primitive tent sites set among dense subalpine fir.

Shortly after leaving the campground, the trail tops a rise and offers a panoramic view of Slide Lake and the barren peaks beyond. Yellow and Gable mountains flank the lake to the south and north, and the rounded summit of Seward Mountain can be seen to the south of a more jagged, unnamed peak which lies at the head of the valley. A trail once ran up the valley above Slide Lake to an old mine site, but the trail has been long abandoned and can no longer be followed.

Gable Pass Option. From the lower end of Slide Lake, the Gable Pass trail ascends to the north, climbing up forested benches and along boulder-filled ravines to the summit of Gable Pass. A short bushwhack up the ridgeline to the east is rewarded by panoramic views of the Belly River country to the north, as well as the tortured forms of the mountains flanking the pass.

From Gable Pass, the trail passes around the base of Gable Mountain, through alpine parkland inhabited by numerous rodents and songbirds. The

Papoose from Gable Pass.

trail is difficult to follow in places but rock cairns have been built to guide hikers across the rocky area.

The trail passes the junction with the Lee Ridge trail, a poorly maintained trail that runs northward along a gentle ridge to its intersection with the Chief Mountain Highway. From this point, the trail descends into lodgepole pine forest and continues downward fairly steeply until it emerges behind the Belly River Ranger Station.

CONNECTING TRAILS

A secondary trail runs up the wooded crest of **Lee Ridge** from mile 17.8 of the Chief Mountain Highway. The trail is not a primary one but can be followed fairly easily as it winds through pine and spruce forests below the west face of Chief Mountain to connect with the Gable Pass trail .3 mile west of the pass.

The North Fork trail. A primitive trail runs north from Threemile campground for 4.8 miles to reach the North Fork of the Belly River. It climbs across a wooded hillside before winding around the east flank of Sentinel

Mountain and descending into the North Fork valley. An old trail used to run up this valley to its head at Miche Wabun Lake but has been abandoned for years and now exists only on unrevised topographic maps.

The **Belly-Mokowanis cutoff** trail runs from the foot of Cosley Lake to a point on the Belly River just below Dawn Mist Falls. For hikers traveling from Goat Haunt to the upper Belly River valley, this trail eliminated unnecessary distance by "cutting the corner" over the shoulder of Natoas Peak instead of following the drainage patterns. You must wade the outlet of Cosley Lake; a wire is strung across the creek for stability.

EXTENDED TRIPS

The trail system in Glacier National Park is composed of miles of interlinked trails which allow the adventurous backpacker an almost infinite array of choices. Outlined below are a few recommended routes for travelers wishing to escape for longer than a couple of days. Travelers are reminded that back-country permits are issued for a maximum of six nights. For extended trips, it is especially important to ascertain trail conditions before leaving and also to prepare for all types of weather conditions. The mountains reward those who come prepared, but are frequently unforgiving to those who tempt the fates. By playing it safe, wise hikers ensure that they will have an enjoyable trip.

THE CONTINENTAL DIVIDE NATIONAL SCENIC TRAIL

Marias Pass to Canadian Border
Allow 10 days

The trail: The Continental Divide National Scenic Trail, authorized by congress in 1968, follows a 3,100-mile route along the spine of the continent from Mexico to the Canadian border. The segment of the trail running through Glacier National Park was designated in 1988 and originates at Marias Pass and runs through the heart of the park, following well-maintained trails that feature spectacular views of Glacier's diverse wildlands.

The Continental Divide Trail enters the park at a trailhead located at the summit of Marias Pass on U.S. Highway 2. The route follows this spur trail to a junction with the **Autumn Creek Trail**, which it follows eastward all the way to the town of East Glacier. From East Glacier, the route hooks up with the trail to **Scenic Point**, which exits town behind the golf course. This trail ascends steadily to a summit at Scenic Point, from which sweeping views of the high plains can be taken in on a clear day. The trail descends steeply to a trailhead on the Two Medicine Road, at which point the hiker should turn left, following the road for a quarter mile to the Two Medicine campground.

From the campground, the route crosses a footbridge and heads up the Dry Fork valley to Pitamakan Pass (see **Dawson-Pitamakan** trail). From this high point, the trail descends steadily into the **Cutbank Creek** valley, past Pitamakan and Morningstar lakes to a junction with the trail to **Triple Divide Pass**. Turning west here, the Continental Divide Trail ascends steadily to the aforementioned pass, then descends quickly to the head of the Hudson Bay Creek drainage, which it follows to **Red Eagle Lake.** Several miles beyond the foot of the lake, the route turns west again at a trail junction that leads the hiker to the south shore of **St. Mary Lake.**

The trail runs westward along the lakeshore for about ten miles, passing Virginia Falls and reaching St. Mary Falls. Upon crossing the St. Mary River, turn west for the **Piegan Pass** trail, which follows the valley floor for 1.4 miles and then ascends steadily up the north wall of the valley, eventually

EXTENDED TRIPS

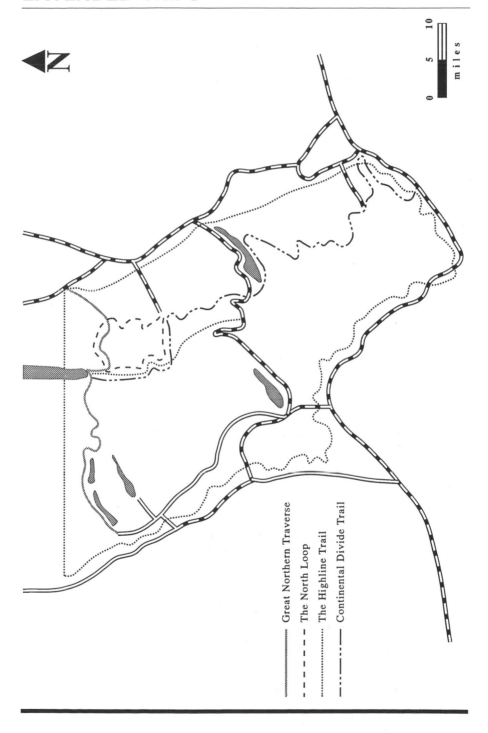

N

0 5 10
miles

Great Northern Traverse
The North Loop
The Highline Trail
Continental Divide Trail

crossing the Going-to-the-Sun Road. After crossing the highway, follow the signs to Piegan Pass as the trail passes beneath the western flanks of Going-to-the-Sun Mountain. After reaching the pass, the trail descends, and the hiker should keep right to follow the quickest route to the Many Glacier Hotel.

From this point, an alternate route runs over **Redgap Pass** and descends into the **Belly River** valley, ending up at Chief Mountain Customs on State Highway 17. The primary route resumes at the Swiftcurrent Motor Lodge and heads westward, ascending steeply to **Swiftcurrent Pass.** Once over the pass, the route reaches the **Highline Trail** at Granite Park Chalets. From here, it is comparatively easy going along the Continental Divide to Fifty Mountain campground, where the trail drops steeply into the **Waterton Valley**. This trail terminates at Goat Haunt Ranger Station, from which hikers can either take a ferry to Waterton townsite in Canada or continue the trek around the western shore of Waterton Lake, reaching the town by trail. Either way, hikers entering Canada will have to pass through customs.

THE GREAT NORTHERN TRAVERSE

Kintla Lake to Chief Mountain customs
Allow 6 days

The trail: This route encompasses some of the wildest and most scenic terrain in the park and affords a strenuous challenge to the serious backpacker. The trail begins at Kintla Lake, on the trail to **Boulder Pass**. The first twelve miles are an easy stroll along the shores of Kintla and Upper Kintla lakes, where views are limited by the density of the forest. Beyond Upper Kintla Lake, the trail begins a grueling ascent to Boulder Pass as the views begin to open up, exposing the majestic peaks on all sides. After passing through Boulder Pass, the trail descends around the Hole in the Wall cirque and then drops further to Brown Pass. A relatively easy descent lands the hiker in the Olsen Creek valley, which the trail follows through the trees to the junction with the **Waterton Lake** trail.

From this junction, the hiker should follow the trail signs to Goat Haunt Ranger Station, on the south shore of Waterton Lake. From the ranger station, the route heads south, following the **Waterton Valley** beneath the boles of old-growth conifers. After topping a brief rise, the route meets a junction with the **Stoney Indian Pass** trail, which it follows eastward again, rising into open meadows and rocky fields. The summit of this pass rewards the hiker with more fantastic vistas of glacier-carved pinnacles before descending past numerous waterfalls into the Mokowanis River Valley. A gentle descent past a chain of lakes takes the traveler to a junction with the **Belly River** trail. Just to the north is a seasonally manned ranger station, while the primary route takes the hiker northward, following the meanders of the Belly River through meadows and copses toward the Chief Mountain Customs. The last several miles are a surprisingly steep and strenuous ascent up a hillside to the trail's terminus; save some energy for this final push.

THE HIGHLINE TRAIL

Logan Pass to Goat Haunt R.S.
Allow 3 days.

The trail: This trail is popular because it allows easy access to the high country without requiring pass-climbing heroics or special wilderness skills. The easiest routing is to hike the trail from south to north, as this avoids a grueling ascent up the southern wall of the Waterton Valley. The trail begins at Logan Pass and runs below the crest of the **Garden Wall** to Granite Park Chalets, which offers beds and hot meals to travelers with reservations. For those who prefer to camp, a nearby campground is reserved especially for hikers on extended trips during most of the season.

From Granite Park, the route continues north, following the **Northern Highline** as it descends and then rises again on its way to Fifty Mountain campground. The route then descends steeply down an open hillside to the shaded depths of the **Waterton Valley**, which it follows to its terminus at Goat Haunt Ranger Station. A nearby boat dock provides shuttle service to Waterton townsite for a modest fee. The adventurous traveler may also decide to follow the trail around the western shore of Waterton Lake, which provides a longer route to this Canadian destination.

THE NORTH CIRCLE

Loop begins and terminates at Swiftcurrent Motor Lodge
Allow 5 days

The trail: The North Circle is a traditional routing for backpackers who wish to sample the charms of the Belly River country. Although three major passes are crossed, this route is suitable for intermediate-level backpackers, and a wealth of campgrounds along the way make more extended visits possible. The route follows the **Ptarmigan Tunnel** trail northward from Swiftcurrent to a junction with the **Iceberg Lake** trail; a side trip to Iceberg Lake is well worth the effort. From this junction, the primary route runs northward past the barren tarn of Ptarmigan Lake to the Ptarmigan Tunnel, which cuts through a sheer rock wall and allows passage into the Belly River country beyond.

After the tunnel, spectacular views open up on the long descent to Elizabeth Lake. From the shore of this favored fishing spot, the trail follows the **Belly River** northward to the Dawn Mist Falls. Shortly after this milestone, a connecting trail that cuts off to the west brings the traveler across a ford below Cosley Lake to the **Stoney Indian Pass** trail. Here the trail turns southwest, passing a chain of lakes that offer fine opportunities for the fisherman. After reaching the head of Glenns Lake, the trail ascends past tumbling waterfalls to the heights of Stoney Indian Pass. A foot-pounding descent brings the hiker to the foot of the **Waterton Valley**, where the route turns southward and begins a toilsome ascent up open slopes to the meadowy expanses of the Fifty Mountain area.

From Fifty Mountain campground, the route continues southward on the **Northern Highline**, descending slightly and then ascending again before reaching Granite Park. At this juncture, hikers completing the loop should turn east, taking the easy route over **Swiftcurrent Pass**. After the pass is reached, views of the Swiftcurrent Valley are revealed along the steep descent to the valley floor. The last few miles are an almost imperceptible descent past dwarfed aspens and shallow lakes to the original starting point.

For Further Reading

Available from the Glacier Natural History Association:

Place Names of Waterton-Glacier National Park, Holterman. 170 pp. (Glacier Natural History Association Publication)

Mammals of the Northern Rockies, Ulrich. 160 pp. (Mountain Press)

Bear Attacks: Their Causes and Avoidance. Herrero. 286 pp. (Lyons and Burford)

Birds of the Northern Rockies. Ulrich. 160 pp. (Mountain Press)

Natural History Pamphlet Series. (Glacier Natural History Association Publication)
About Bears, Day Hikes, Fish & Fishing, Glaciers & Glaciation, Kings of the Mountain (Mountain Goats & Big Horn Sheep), and Wolves of Glacier.

Plants of Waterton-Glacier National Parks and the Northern Rockies. Shaw and On. 160 pp. (Mountain Press)

Along the Trail. Summer and On. 114 pp. (Glacier Natural History Association Publication)

Climber's Guide to Glacier National Park. Edwards. 347 pp. (Glacier Natural History Association Publication)

Fishing Glacier National Park. Hintzen. (Glacier Natural History Association Publication)

Three Forks of the Flathead. 36 pp. (Glacier Natural History Association Publication)

Jewel Basin Hiking Map. Flathead National Forest. 18" x 18". (Glacier Natural History Association Publication)

USGS Topographic Map of Glacier National Park. 41" x 38". (US Geological Survey)

Topographic Quadrangle Maps for Glacier National Park. Scale 1:24,000. (US Geological Survey)

Many Storied Mountains. Beaumont. 138 pp. (National Park Service)

APPENDIX I:
FISHING OPPORTUNITIES

Fish Species
BKT - Brook Trout
BTR - Bull Trout
GRY - Grayling
LKT - Lake Trout
RBT - Rainbow Trout
WCT - West Slope Cutthroat Trout
WTF - Whitefish
YCT - Yellowstone Cutthroat Trout
KOK - Kokanee (landlocked sockeye salmon)

Fishing Quality
VG - Very Good
G - Good
F - Fair
P - Poor

	Fish Species	*Quality*	*Comments*
Streams			
Belly River	GRY, RBT	P	
Lower McDonald Creek	WCT	F	Catch & Release
Middle Fork Flathead	BTR, WCT	P	
Midvale Creek	RBT, BKT	G	
North Fork Flathead	BTR, WCT	F	
Red Eagle Creek	RBT	F	
Two Medicine Creek	BKT, RBT	F	
Lakes			
Avalanche	WCT	F	
Cosley	RBT	G	
Elizabeth	RBT, GRY	VG	
Ellen Wilson	BKT	VG	
Francis	RBT	G	
Glenns	RBT, WTF, BKT	F	
Grace	WCT	VG	
Gunsight	RBT	VG	
Hidden	WCT	F	
Isabel	RBT	VG	
Josephine	BKT, KOK	F	
Lincoln	WCT, BKT	F	
Logging	WCT	F	
McDonald	LKT, WCT, WTF	P	
Mokowanis	BKT	G	
Oldman	YCT	G	
Quartz	RBT, WCT	F	
Red Eagle	RBT, WCT, BKT	G	
Slide	BTR	F	
St. Mary	RBT, WTF	F	
Swiftcurrent	BKT, KOK	F	
Trout	WCT, RBT	F	Flyfishing Only
Two Medicine	BKT, RBT	F	

APPENDIX II: BACKCOUNTRY CAMPGROUND TABLE

Ratings
5 - campground is a scenic attraction in itself.
4 - campground in an area of high scenic value.
3 - campground in an area of moderate scenic value.
2 - campground in an area with low scenic value.

Comments
1 - One night stay limit July and August.
2 - Extended trips only.
3 - Open June 1 to September 11, when launch is running.
4 - May not be scheduled for first night of trip.
5 - Special approval required.

Campground Name	Rating	Sites	Fires	Horses	Comment
Adair Lake	3	4	yes	6	
Akokala Lake	3	3	no	no	
Arrow Lake	4	2	no	5	
Atlantic Creek	2	4	yes	6	
Beaver Woman Lake	2	2	yes	10	
*Belly River R.S.	2	4	yes	no	
Boulder Pass	5	3	no	no	
Bowman Lake, Head	3	6	yes	10	
Brown Pass	3	3	no	no	
Camas Lake	3	2	no	no	
*Coal Creek	2	2	yes	10	
Cobalt Lake	3	2	no	no	1
Cosley Lake	3	4	yes	6	
Cracker Lake	5	3	no	no	
Elizabeth Lake, Foot	4	6	no	8	
*Elizabeth Lake, Head	2	3	yes	6	1
Fifty Mountain	4	5	no	6	
Flattop	3	3	no	6	
Glenns Lake, Foot	3	4	yes	8	
Glenns Lake, Head	4	3	yes	no	
*Goat Haunt Shelters	3	7	yes	no	3
Grace Lake	4	3	yes	no	
Granite Park	5	4	no	no	1, 2
Gunsight Lake	4	8	no	10	
Harrison Lake	3	3	yes	6	
*Hawksbill	3	2	no	no	
Helen Lake	3	2	no	no	

Campground Name	Rating	Sites	Fires	Horses	Comment
Hole in the Wall	5	5	no	no	
Kintla Lake, Head	2	6	yes	10	
Kootenai Lake	3	4	no	5	
*Lake Frances	4	2	no	no	
Lake Isabel	4	2	yes	no	
Lake Janet	1	2	yes	6	
Lincoln Lake	5	3	no	8	
Lake Ellen Wilson	4	4	no	5	1
Logging Lake, Foot	4	4	yes	no	
*Lower Nyack	2	2	yes	10	
Lower Quartz Lake	3	4	yes	6	
Many Glacier	4	2	yes	no	1, 2, 4
McDonald Lake	3	2	no	no	
Mokowanis Lake	4	2	no	no	
*Mokowanis Junction	2	5	yes	8	
Morning Star	4	3	no	no	
No Name Lake	4	3	no	no	1
Oldman Lake	4	4	no	5	1
Ole Creek	2	3	yes	8	
*Ole Lake	3	2	yes	5	
Otokomi Lake	3	3	no	no	
Park Creek	2	3	yes	6	
Poia Lake	3	4	no	10	
Quartz Lake, Foot	4	3	no	no	
*Red Eagle, Head	3	4	yes	10	
Red Eagle, Foot	4	4	yes	no	
Reynolds Creek	3	1	yes	10	5
Slide Lake	2	2	yes	5	
Snyder Lake	4	3	no	5	
*Sperry	3	4	no	no	1
Stoney Indian Lake	5	3	no	no	
Three Mile	2	3	yes	6	
Upper Kintla Lake	4	4	yes	10	
Upper Nyack	4	2	yes	10	
*Upper Park Creek	3	3	yes	6	
Upper Two Medicine	5	4	no	no	1
Waterton River	2	5	yes	6	

ABOUT THE AUTHORS

Author Erik Molvar.

Erik Molvar discovered backpacking while cooking on a volunteer trail crew in the North Cascades of Washington. A newfound taste for the wilderness experience inspired him to choose a career in the outdoors, and he soon found himself at the University of Montana pursuing a Bachelor's degree in wildlife biology. Montana's craggy ranges were to be his weekend playground for the next five years, and two summers of bartending at Lake McDonald Lodge gave Erik the perfect opportunity to fully explore Glacier National Park's backcountry. An adventurous spirit has led Erik to embark upon backpacking expeditions throughout the Rocky Mountains, the Great Basin, western Canada, and Alaska. While writing this book, Erik was studying moose behavior in Alaska on the way to a Master's degree, and plotting his return to the Big Sky country.

Matthew Cutler grew up pursuing trout and elk in the high country of his native Utah. An inborn taste for the outdoors and the call of unspoiled wilderness lured Matt to Glacier as a seasonal concessions worker. Matt's peakbagging talents and native good humor have added immeasurably to the experiences of his backcountry companions through the years.

Candice Hanson is a naturalized Montanan who has dedicated herself to a rigorous outdoor life. Originally from the Dakotas, Candy forsook the flatlands to become a ranger in Glacier National Park. She rounds out her year by working at the Big Mountain Ski Resort in Whitefish, Montana.

The authors feel honored to share their firsthand knowledge and insights with those less familiar with Glacier's delights. Between these three, thousands of miles have passed underfoot, including all of the major trails of Glacier country. It is their hope that this book will serve as a window into Glacier's many-faceted beauty, enticing those who read it to leave the cares of the world behind and lose themselves in the majesty of the mountains.

Glacier Natural History Association

The Glacier Natural History Association was organized in 1946. This nonprofit group cooperates with the National Park Service by assisting the Interpretive Division of Glacier National Park. Together they develop broad public understanding of the geology, plant and animal life, history, and related subjects of the park region. In recent years the Association has expanded its activities to serve the needs of additional agencies, such as the National Bison Range, the Grant-Kohrs National Historic Site, the Big Hole National Battlefield, and the Flathead National Forest.

Anyone wishing to support the goals and activities of the Association may become a member. Members receive a 15% discount on purchases from the Association and similar discounts from many cooperating associations in other national park areas. They also receive the Association's newsletter and annual report and may attend the annual meeting, as well as any special meetings, and vote on the Board of Directors and any questions addressed at the meetings. Also, from time to time the Association offers special items for sale to members only.

For information on membership and dues, please contact: Glacier Natural History Association, Box 428, West Glacier, MT 59936, or call (406) 888-5756.

HIKING NOTES

HIKING NOTES

HIKING NOTES

HIKING NOTES

FALCON GUIDES

★ *Starred titles are new in the* **FALCON** GUIDES *series.*

★ Angler's Guide to Alaska	$ 9.95
Angler's Guide to Montana	$ 9.95
Back Country Byways	$ 9.95
Beartooth Fishing Guide	$ 7.95
Floater's Guide to Colorado	$11.95
★ Floater's Guide to Missouri	$ 9.95
Floater's Guide to Montana	$ 8.95
★ Hiker's Guide to Alaska	$ 9.95
★ Hiker's Guide to Alberta	$ 9.95
Hiker's Guide to Arizona (revised)	$ 9.95
Hiker's Guide to California (revised)	$11.95
Hiker's Guide to Colorado (revised)	$11.95
Hiker's Guide to Hot Springs in the Pacific NW	$ 9.95
Hiker's Guide to Idaho (revised)	$11.95
Hiker's Guide to Montana (revised)	$ 9.95
Hiker's Guide to Montana's Continental Divide Trail	$ 9.95
Hiker's Guide to Nevada	$ 9.95
Hiker's Guide to New Mexico	$ 9.95
★ Hiker's Guide to Oregon	$ 9.95
★ Hiker's Guide to Texas	$ 9.95
Hiker's Guide to Utah (revised)	$11.95
★ Hiker's Guide to Virginia	$ 9.95
Hiker's Guide to Washington	$ 9.95
★ Hiker's Guide to Wyoming	$ 9.95
Hunter's Guide to Montana	$ 9.95
Recreation Guide to California National Forests	$ 9.95
Rockhound's Guide to Montana	$ 7.95
Scenic Byways	$ 9.95
★ Scenic Byways II	$ 9.95
★ Trail of the Great Bear	$12.95
★ Trail Guide to Glacier National Park	$ 9.95
★ Virginia Scenic Drives	$ 9.95

Falcon Press Publishing Co.–call toll-free 1-800-582-2665